Baptized in Dirty Water

Short Theological Engagements with Popular Music

Short Theological Engagements with Popular Music features theologians who have a passion for particular popular artists and who offer robust theological engagements with the work of that artist—engaging a song, an album, or a whole body of work over a career. Books in the series are accessible, yet deep both in their theological and musical engagement. Each book foregrounds ideas of interest in the musician's work, first, and puts these into conversation with the context and culture, second, and the Christian tradition, third. Each book, therefore, includes analysis of the cultural artifact, cultural context, and the relation to Christian tradition. Each book endeavors, as well, to speak with vitality to the challenges of living with God's mercy and justice in today's world.

Baptized in Dirty Water

Reimagining the Gospel according to
TUPAC AMARU SHAKUR

Daniel White Hodge

CASCADE *Books* • Eugene, Oregon

BAPTIZED IN DIRTY WATER
Reimagining the Gospel according to Tupac Amaru Shakur

Short Theological Engagements with Popular Music

Cascade Books
An Imprint of Wipf and Stock Publishers
199 W. 8th Ave., Suite 3
Eugene, OR 97401

www.wipfandstock.com

PAPERBACK ISBN: 978-1-5326-1366-1
HARDCOVER ISBN: 978-1-5326-1368-5
EBOOK ISBN: 978-1-5326-1367-8

Cataloguing-in-Publication data:

Names:White Hodge, Daniel.

Title: Baptized in dirty water : reimagining the gospel according to Tupac Amaru Shakur / by Daniel White Hodge..

Description: Eugene, OR: Cascade Books, 2019 | Series: Short Theological Engagements with Popular Music | Includes bibliographical references.

Identifiers: ISBN 978-1-5326-1366-1 (paperback) | ISBN 978-1-5326-1368-5 (hardcover) | ISBN 978-1-5326-1367-8 (ebook)

Subjects: LCSH: Shakur, Tupac, 1971–1996. | Religion and cuture. | Popular music—Religious aspects. | Rap (music)

Classification: ML3930.S48 W55 2019 (paperback) | ML3930.S48 (ebook)

.　　04/18/19

Contents

Tables and Figures

Introduction

The Hip Hop Theologian and Thinker, Tupac

I'd be remiss if I didn't say I wasn't biased and could objectively explore the topic of Tupac Shakur and his theological pursuits. The academic quest in the West tends to manufacture a sense of disembodiment from research, yet who of us can truly do that with an honest shake? The current sociopolitical era we find ourselves here in the US, in the early part of the twenty-first century, is a nefarious one and one that pits itself against people of color (PoC)—particularly Black and Latinx bodies. The legacy of Tupac's ideology, worldview, theology, and even "sins," have never been needed more. Thus, it is difficult to objectively look at Tupac as an Afro-Latinx male living in the Midwest at a time when I could be killed for simply looking suspicious. Tupac creates a space to lament. Tupac can transcend time and connect with current events. Tupac was prophetic in his approach to life—and not just in his music. Tupac's vigor and energy for life, especially Black life, is needed and is something that a new ethnic-minority generation, growing up in a post-civil rights context, needs to connect with.

Let me situate this in another way. As I sit writing this book, the current time, context, climate, and culture in the United States is fraught with racial, gender, and cultural strain the likes of which have not been seen since the Jim Crow era. It is a time unlike any other. While the period prior to the 1970s was direct and intense racism, the present context utilizes social media, passive- and micro-aggression to create its hegemony and culture of hate. I struggle as a racially Black male living in the US and trying to live out a faith rooted in Christianity—particularly when the history of Christianity has been shown to be objectionable to not only the color of my skin, but my narrative, body, and life.[1] The events that have taken the main stage in media's public sphere started to erupt, at least personally, during the Troy Davis campaign. Here, a young Black male, who was convicted of shooting and killing a White police officer, sat on death row. When I began to research the issue and Davis' case, I found that little physical evidence for him was actually found and the "eyewitness" later recanted the story of seeing Davis murder the police officer.[2] Amid a strong social media campaign and even phone calls to elected officials, Troy Davis was executed on September 21, 2011. Then came Trayvon Martin and later Michael Brown,[3] then both the Ferguson and Baltimore

1. One must consider the use of Christianity as both a racist and violent tool of oppression toward many Africans and African Americans—not to mention other ethnic-minority groups such as Mexicans, Chinese, Japanese, and Native Americans. This will be engaged more later in this text as it relates to missions and colonialization.

2. I do realize this is a controversial case; in fact, most Black and White cases typically are. From my research and investigation, Troy Davis should have had another trial and the new evidence should have been admitted into that trial. I am fully aware that many White evangelicals took issue with the Davis trial and sided with the courts. This is part of the ongoing tensions in the US and especially in Christian evangelical circles.

3. This is in no way minimizing the women and other Black youth who have been murdered and/or killed at the hands of either police officers or "vigilante" White citizens. What I suggest here are the capstone events that have shaped both our nation and where I personally stand as a Black Christian male.

uprisings, and then the terrorist acts of Dylann Roof in Charleston, South Carolina. Roof mercilessly murdered nine Black church members of the historic Emmanuel AME Church. Tamir Rice, Dante Parker, John Crawford III, Sandra Bland, and in Chicago, Laquan McDonald. This list could continue with names as it seems the killing of Black bodies has become an epidemic sport the US. All of which Christian discourse is used to continue the subjugation of Black bodies, in the use of "forgive," "love your enemies," "bless those that curse you." And while in allegory, at least, those are hoped for and desired, the reality is that when White America feels threatened or is attacked (e.g., 9/11), the opposite of those replies is taken and a type of "holy violence" is often utilized.[4] While I see White evangelical youth dancing to Lecrae at one of his concerts, the irony comes when those same youth tell me things like "Michael Brown wasn't innocent and probably deserved to die." Or "These 'thugs' were asking for it." Or the classic, "This was part of God's plan."[5] They say such things as they enjoy and embrace Black culture.

Further, the events that culminated on November 8, 2016, shook many of us in the ethnic-minority community

4. The use of violence and the construct of a "just God" is a matter we will be engaged with briefly in this text, for a greater examination see Hodge, *Hip Hop's Hostile Gospel*, 122–47.

5. These are all direct quotes taken from two summer youth events in 2014 and 2015. The latter quote came from George Zimmerman's interview with Sean Hannity (2012) in which he stated that the killing of Trayvon was part of "God's plan" and that he would "pray for them [Martin's family] daily." This type of discourse is common and is part of the ideological structure that many post-civil rights millennials refuse to engage with and/or adopt. This has ramifications for Evangelicalism as many in the post-civil rights millennial generation view Evangelicals as outdated, racist, sexist, and having a very skewed reality of who "god" is.

when Donald J. Trump was elected as the 45th president of the United States.[6] The election of such a figure in the office of presidency sent a direct message to ethnic-minority communities that their voice did not matter.[7] Our foretold "hope" of the Obama legacy was shown to be mythological in nature and the optimism that was of the coming "demographical changes,"[8] in which minorities were to

6. While the goal here is not to condemn those who favor a conservative perspective, it is, however, important to note that Trump's rhetoric, policies, and many of his appointed cabinet members are aligned with an Alt-Right worldview, which is in direct contradiction to any social justice or intercultural work. Therefore, it is difficult to entertain the notion of Trump being "for all Americans" when it is clear, by his actions and cabinet, that he is only for the continuation of Whiteness as a standard for "American." I would challenge anyone who voted for Trump to defend someone like Stephen Bannon, for example, and the rhetoric of hate he has spewed over the years toward Jews, Blacks, Palestinians, and even women, or that his perspective fits as a "Christian worldview." It is imperative that we critically wrestle with these matters because they are of utmost importance for anyone who regards Christianity as their faith.

7. It is also noted in emerging research that the presence and notion of "growing diversity" creates fear in many Whites who concern themselves with the changing electorate. This also illustrates the fear that has existed in many White churches for decades regarding growing ethnic-minority populations. See Major, Blodorn, and Major Blascovich, "Threat of Increasing Diversity." A type of warning, if you will, was issued in the classic text by Emerson and Smith, *Divided by Faith,* which, even then, outlined the growing gap within Evangelical churches.

8. Those who are rooted in the notion that somehow the rise of ethnic-minority population in the US will somehow skew voting to reflect a more "diverse" country and one that has an emphasis on social justice. While no one can accurately predict the future and I too would argue that possibly in two or three generations we may very well be in such a locale within the US, as of now, it is not the case, and if we have learned anything from the history of South Africa, we know that those in power do not have to have the majority in ethnic numbers.

finally have triumph and take "power" for justice was just another neoliberal delusion. It also shook those of us who have dedicated our lives to intercultural and racial justice work that 81 percent of White Evangelicals voted for such a person like Trump and continue to support his policies.[9] That was an awakening for me and it made me question the work I do. Had it mattered? Did any of it sink in? How could all the material published and spoken on just go ignored?

All these questions developed while attempting to write this book. My heart is heavy and my mind full. So, I can't sit in a completely objective stance as a researcher, scholar, and professor; my Blackness demands of me much more.

The goal here, then, is to examine a Rap artist and Hip Hop mogul that I would argue presents a way forward theologically. Tupac is not presenting a three-point sermonette with actionized solutions; in fact, Tupac would attempt to complicate the context a bit, rather than provide some type of solution that was much too simplistic. Yet, in that complexity something greater is at work; a fundamental attempt to find God in a contextualized manner and pushing away from colonized White Christianity. Tupac was after God's premise and wanted to better his community, along with attempting to raise the consciousness of that community. But what made Tupac such a prophetic voice and Hip Hop prophet was something that most overlook in prophets, their faults and shortcomings. Tupac was in no way, shape, or form perfect. He didn't have the cadence of an MLK, nor did he possess the seminarian education of a Howard Thurman. Tupac had an image of

9. See Smith and Martínez, "How the Faithful Voted"; Renaud, "Myths Debunked."

a street "hoodlum" within the media. Tupac had charges brought against him on rape. Tupac, despite all his endeavors to uplift women, still fell prey to hypermasculinity and male bravado. Tupac was, at times, a "hot-head" and to his own admittance, spoke before he thought about what he was going to say. In many ways, how can someone like this be a prophet? I think in many ways, this is precisely what makes him prophetic; the intersections of the sacred, secular, and profane are, for me, the space in which God inhabits the most. For someone like Tupac, this was a constant intersection he found himself in; sometimes too profane, sometimes too secular, and, at times, least likely seen in the public as too sacred for even his own good.

Tupac Amaru Shakur.[10] Even the name causes many Hip Hoppers like Kendrick Lamar to stand still and pause for a moment. When asked what he did on hearing the news of Tupac's death, Marlon Wayans stated that he cried like his momma cried when Marvin Gaye was murdered. Young girls and boys who were not even alive during Tupac's life remember and adore him as if they had grown up in his era. Further, even mildly liberal parents today (who were teens in the 1990s) pause and think about the effect Tupac had on their own lives.[11] Tupac was iconic. Recalling Tupac's accomplishments at such a young age, Quincy Jones recalls his death by stating that if Martin Luther King Jr. had died when he was twenty-five, he would have been

10. I must note that fifteen of the interviewees noted that Biggie Smalls was also to be considered a prophet and Hip Hop spiritualist. Only releasing a total of four albums (which pales in comparison to Tupac's arsenal of albums), Biggie is still noted as one of Hip Hop's moguls attempting to work out the profane and secular in sacred spaces. More research is needed on the spiritual significance of Biggie.

11. As seen in my 2004–08 interviews on Tupac's theological mystique in Hodge, *Heaven Has a Ghetto*.

a struggling Black Baptist minister. Malcolm X would have been a street hustler, and Jones himself would have been a struggling trumpet player. When Tupac died at twenty-five, he left a legacy of life, love, rage, pain—and theology. "Tupac was touched by God, not very many people are touched by the hand of God."[12]

Another phenomenon that arises with Tupac is the fact that his music remains a central force within Hip Hop culture. In a music genre that has a bench life of four to six months before it is considered "old-school," Tupac's music remains "new" for many, and it is not uncommon to hear his music (that dates over two decades) played in car stereo systems throughout global cities. Tupac continues to have his presence felt not only within the 'hood, but also in suburbs and rural areas too.

Tupac's audience changed drastically right when he was coming into his own as an artist. In 1992, the artist and producer Dr. Dre released his now infamous album "The Chronic." That was the first commercialized Hip Hop album to be sold primarily to White and affluent youth and marketed outside the 'hood.[13] This monumental date took Hip Hop into the living rooms of upper middle class American homes. For one of the first times, White and affluent youth were gaining a deeper understanding of Black culture, including Tupac's portrayal of Black urban culture.[14]

12. Interview taken from Spirer, *Thug Angel.*

13. See the sales statistics and the projected demographics that this album was marketed to by studying Sound Scan documents and Dr. Dre's album on http://www.allmusic.com/.

14. The word "Black" will be capitalized in this book. The capitalized word refers to the ethnic group African Americans. When the word is in lowercase it will refer to the color black.

Tupac's music was not only attractive to Black and Latinx youth, but also to White youth.[15] Tupac's music reached an even broader audience. Tupac attained iconic status with his murder on September 13, 1996. His image as a ghetto saint went from theoretical to real, and rumors of him still being alive began to grow. Even today, there are groups of people who believe that he is still alive and is planning his return to the music scene. This mystical eschaton of him being alive is about connecting with this hyper-realism that Tupac creates; if Pac is still alive, then, maybe, there is hope. Further, if he is alive, he is a God, for who else has overcome death and come back to life?

Tupac embodied both the theological and the profane, while still embodying a Christological persona that permeated much of his art. This is one reason why so many today still adore him. More importantly, Tupac was a man of his word; he was credible. When he spoke of 'hood violence, you knew he had lived it, "been there, and done that." Teresa Reed states:

> Tupac's experiences afforded him the credentials to preach about the social decay that gave rise to his tragic and famous persona. While Marvin Gaye could sing about war, he had never actually been on a battlefield, on the front line, in the direct line of fire. Tupac, on the other hand, had been there. His descriptions of ghetto life are so disarmingly graphic because they are often his accounts of situations he knew of firsthand.[16]

15. The word "White" will be capitalized in this book. The capitalized word refers to the ethnic group commonly referred to as Anglo, Caucasian, or Euro American. When the word is in lowercase it will refer to the color white.

16. Reed, *Holy Profane*.

Tupac had lived a life that matched the life of his listener. Even if the listener was White and lived in the suburbs, he could still relate to certain elements—be it the party, the money, or the women.

Tupac argued for a spiritual revolution and for community building. Tupac was concerned with 'hood matters and for 'hood youth—Black, Latino, White, Asian, and women. In that same vein, many women loved Tupac. Tupac was both a father and sex image to them. Tupac was also concerned with social justice and for bettering the community as a whole, righting social injustices, bettering the person, helping the young, and gaining wisdom from the older generation.[17] Tupac connected with people and gave to people out of his heart. This was evident in his connection to the audience and how the audience would respond to him during a concert or in public. To take this a step further, Tupac would frequent clubs without security and would just be "hanging out." This was something that made him an even more popular figure—someone who was powerful and popular, but could "hang" with the normal people.

He was iconic in his style, life, language, and messages. Tupac lived the life he talked about[18] and was true to his word. Further, Michael Eric Dyson, in the documentary *Tupac Vs.*, discusses how Tupac's music was like Gospel music; he lived the life he talked about in his music. If you are a gospel singer, this is great, but if you are a rapper,

17. His activism also took place through his wallet and connection to his fan base. Tupac was a giver and one dedicated to the community; his fan base was well aware of this which added to his likability as an artist (Stark, *Future of Religion*). Tupac was a community activist, but many did not know this because the media typically followed Tupac only when he was in trouble.

18. For a deeper understanding of this see Peters, *Tupac Vs.*

then it becomes a problem, being further complicated if you are considered a "gangsta rapper." Moreover, Tupac was one of the few rappers who put meaning and passion to every one of his songs. Most artists have two or three tracks they really work on, and the rest of the album is just filler music. But Tupac put his heart and soul into every song. More importantly, each one of his songs told a story and had purpose.[19]

Michael Eric Dyson states,

> Tupac is perhaps the representative figure of his generation. In his haunting voice can be heard the buoyant hopefulness and the desperate hopelessness that mark the outer perimeters of the Hip Hop culture he eagerly embraced, as well as the lives of the millions of youth who admired and adored him.[20]

Further, as one young man put it to me, "This was the realest nigga you could find. I mean, he was a pastor to me. He helped me through some deep shit in my life."[21] This was a consistent theme throughout my research; it can't be ignored.

Michael Datcher, Kwame Alexander, and Mutulu Shakur tell us that "Tupac Amaru Shakur was ours. He presented himself to our generation like a gift offering. No ribbons, no bows, no paper. He came in a plain box and he came opened."[22] Tupac was relevant to many, and gave voice to a generation that for years had been underrepresented: The Hip Hop generation.

19. See Attachment A for a pictorial view of Tupac.
20. Dyson, *Holler If You Hear Me*, 13.
21. See Hodge, *Heaven Has a Ghetto*.
22. Datcher, Alexander, and Shakur, *Tough Love*, introduction.

For me, as someone who is in pursuit of a non-colonized Jesus, I am compelled to study and understand Tupac's theological message. What makes Tupac have a theological message as compared to Kendrick Lamar? Tupac was one of the first rappers to conjoin the profane and the sacred. Tupac's scandalous union of these two concepts made him a controversial figure for some, but also made him a hero for others.

Direction of This Text

So, what am I after here in this book? This series is designed to take a closer look at iconic symbols within pop culture and elaborate more on them and their theological connections. This book is about that. I admittedly struggled to figure out what I was even going to say to begin with. A decade prior I could have written an entire encyclopedia about Tupac and still had material left over. I would pine and beg to get a book contract to write on him. Over the years, the field of Hip Hop studies has grown exponentially; there are a lot of new and great voices speaking on some important areas including hypermasculinity, gender, sexual orientation, intersectionality, and even religion. The sub-field of religion and Hip Hop has seen its growth too. This sub-field did not exist when I began studying Tupac in the early 2000s. In fact, the topic of Hip Hop and religion was almost considered to be an F-word in evangelical circles. The academy was still trying to figure out if Hip Hop was even "worthy enough" to study, much less seminaries having someone do their PhD on Tupacian theology. Yet, over time, there have been individuals who have pioneered new methods, theories, theologies, and boundaries to create the sub-field of religion and Hip Hop within

Hip Hop studies. This is grand. I am proud to say I have been a part of this formation. But what does this have to do with Tupac, you say? Well, quite a bit has been said on Tupac over the last decade and the idea of "Tupac's gospel," while novel and sexy back in 2005, is a bit on the "been there done that" trail. Moreover, with the emergence of Tupac-like rappers such as J. Cole, Kendrick Lamar, Childish Gambino, and even Cardi B (to some extent), there is an entirely new generation of rappers to explore dealing with millennial, Gen Y, and Gen Z issues facing our current context. What might Tupac have to say?

Well, that is where this book comes in. As someone who has spent hours immersed in Tupac's life, poetry, interviews, family structure, and within Hip Hop culture itself, I would like to present a text that is a mile-high view of both the artist and what he brings to this sociopolitical era in which we find ourselves in. The main argument here is that Tupac remains a post-civil rights figure who has inspired and helped generate new artists that are speaking truth to power; Tupac is in pursuit of a non-colonized version of Jesus, which means he is living out the disrupter that Jesus was, historically. Thus, this book situates itself as being a guide to 1) understanding Tupac, 2) the post-civil rights theological approach, and 3) what a Hip Hop Gospel looks like within the context and lens of one of its own, Tupac Amaru Shakur. For you, as the reader, it is my intention to lay the facts out and allow you to make your own conclusions. Yes, as I have already stated, it's difficult to remain unbiased when dealing with such personal issues. There will be times when I'm just preaching, using Pac as the hermeneutic. But, the premise here is to illustrate the complexity of what we call Christianity and to begin to suggest, not tell, a different way forward in the faith outside of White evangelicalism.

That said, there needs to be some break down of what the process here will look like. First, I'd like to take a bit of time explaining what the post-civil rights context is, I think this will lay out the setting of the entire book. I would assume some of you reading this are not familiar with the vast history of Hip Hop culture and even less familiar with the African American diaspora. This is not a bad thing, I mean, you're reading this text, right? But, it does mean that without that context, you'd be kind of lost on some of the language. Second, I think it would be fitting, since many of you have not read my academic text on Tupac published in 2009[23]—which I myself cannot afford. So, that being said, I think it good to figure out the history of Tupac and how he came to be. The man created a cultural revolution by age twenty-five; it would be good to figure out why! Lastly, I'd like to then present my thoughts on why Tupac is a post-civil rights prophet, ending on a description of his post-soul Gospel message. Because we live in a visual world, I've also placed some appendices in this text to highlight some more visual information. I know, I know, appendices are for them four-syllable scholarly-type books. Yes. I get that. What if we just change the language on it then? Let's call them attachments, and let's look at it as a way to get a broader view on the personhood of Tupac. Yes? Okay, good!

This book is intended to spark conversation, not end it. This book is created to give an overview of a specific person, not a detailed academic study. This book is written to catapult the reader into a higher level of learning.

23. See attachment G to see the material used to gather my data . . . it's a good chunk of stuff.

I would undertake that by reading this, you wish to gain both an understanding and knowledge of who Tupac was and how he is situated in the Hip Hop cultural continuum. I would also assume that you have some interest in both Hip Hop and Tupac, along with their connection to Christian theology. Well, then you are in the right place. I do want to say at the outset that I am not here to answer any longing issues. One simply can't do that in a text of this length—or within any given text for that matter. Again, the goal here is to create a dialogue and push the mind forward into a new space of understanding. Tupac has had many things written on him concerning his death, poetry, and his alleged connections to the Illuminati. Yet, very little written on him, text-wise, concerning his theological and/or post-soul pursuits. So, here is this volume to engage in that area.

Oh, and before we get into chapter 1, let me clear two things up since I get asked these questions all the time and I'm sure a lot of you are thinking them right now: 1) no, I do not believe in the Illuminati, nor do I think Tupac was a part of it; and 2) yes, Tupac is dead. There's no way someone like him could have been silent and "off the grid" for two decades.

Okay, now that we've cleared that up, let's dive in!

1

Hip Hop Culture and Context in the Post-civil Rights Era

The opening scene[1] takes us to minstrel caricatures while placing an emphasis to the care of guns over human life; Donald Glover, a.k.a. Childish Gambino, jolts his audience into submission by violently shooting a once artistic person in the head. Glover's use of a warehouse and constant dancers around him remind the audience that Black bodies are entrapped within the US constructs of popular culture and society, yet the focus desires you to be entertained while overlooking the atrocities happening in the background. Glover connects you with an optical artifactual element to the death of Black bodies, police terrorism, the ignorance of White America toward Black America, and the issue of gun violence all in a four-minute video. Glover does not hold back, while a choir sings, meant to represent the nine slain African Americans at Emanuel African Methodist Episcopal Church in Charleston, South Carolina, Glover peaks his head into the room as if to be amused by their song. Then, without cause, he takes an AK-47 and releases several rounds into the choir as you see their blood spatter

1 Childish Gambino, "This is America." https://youtu.be/VYOjWnS4cMY.

against the wall behind them; once again, though, the gun is taken away with care and wrapped carefully. Glover has references to death, as a person with a black hood rides a white horse adjacent to police cars with their lights on. Keep in mind that Glover tells us, "This is a celly, ha; this is a tool, yeah; on my Kodak, woo Black," a stark reference to Stephon Clark's death over a cell phone mistaken for a gun—but do not miss the secondary reference to the young people using their cell phones to film and take pictures of everything around them; from up high, no less. This is a glaring and searing indictment to the transmediated world we are living in that can see Black entertainers as funny, jovial, loud, and humorous, but, on the other end, define them as thugs, miscreants, and even demons if they do not adhere to the "law of the land." Yes, Glover engages with our society's love for violence and disdain for Black bodies within White spaces. The end of the video has Glover running for his life, as if he had figured out the matrix's plan and was now being chased down for it; the people chasing him are out of focus, but it is noted that they are White people attempting to bring him back to the warehouse. Glover connects with his sunken place, and attempts to escape. Can he?

This, is Hip Hop.

The Hip Hop Social Imagination

Hip Hop transcends the mediated tropes of sexualized PoC bodies only yammering for money, fame, fortune, and to "be the best." Hip Hop is much more than tattoos, arpeggiated high hats and snares, gold chains, fancy grills, and baggy pants (albeit that was in the late '90s). No, Hip Hop is a culture, a lifestyle; it is something that we must take into strong consideration and begin to not just analyze for lyrical purposes, but begin to ask what does and can Hip Hop offer theologically and how might it inform our own lives? This is a large part of what Tupac was pursuing. . . . More on that in a bit.

Hip Hop is larger than the radio, commercialized artists, and record industry branding. It is a culture, a people, a movement, a growing community of people that live, breathe, eat, love, hate, and work just as anyone else does. Hip Hop cannot be easily understood or defined. It is complex and full of narratives that would blow away even the strongest anthropologist.[2] Hip Hop, in the words of KRS-One, is "something that is being lived."

I was five years old when I first recognized the power of Hip Hop. I had never heard lyrics, music, and prose that sounded like that. I never realized that an artist could be that direct and open with their artistic style. Moreover, I was made to feel that my own identity was validated in the music and that it was "okay" to be me. Living in a rural town in the center of Texas, one might think that Hip Hop had no reach, but it did. I was able to witness the culture develop from a small group of grassroots artists in the Bronx. By the time I moved to the Bay Area in California, I saw the depth of the Hip Hop community, affectionately referred to as Bay Area Rap. These artists, who emerged onto the public scene, gave a voice to the oppression, anger, and frustration felt by many living in the post-industrial

2. Hip Hop studies is a growing field and therefore I would argue that much more research needs to be done on the sociopolitical, sociosexual tendencies of Hip Hop, how male dominance in the church has affected Hip Hop's view of God, how the LGBTQ community engages God and Rap, how global Rap artists like the Iron Sheik (from Iraq) deconstruct neocolonialism, and how atheism is dealt with within a Hip Hop construct. These are subjects and areas that are worth the time and interdisciplinary study.

urban environment[3] during the crack era.[4] For many, Hip Hop became a discourse vehicle that echoed the concerns, anger, hate, love, pain, hope, vision, anxiety, desire, and joy that had gone unheard in the media. Hip Hop was, as Chuck D once said, "our CNN." It was the voice of a generation. That voice provided a place at the social table for the turmoil being lived out across America's ghettos.[5]

Through Hip Hop, one was able to realize the reprehensible common experience happening in the urban centers, and that one was not alone in that experience; it was a narrative that needed explaining and needed to be told. It was a narrative that would lay the ground for postmodern

3. This phrase was first raised by George, *Post-Soul Nation*, to describe the acute forms of discrimination, oppression, and societal ailments experienced by those living in the inner city during the 1980s. This will be discussed later in chapters 1 and 2.

4. This was the period between 1979 and 1991 for most of the US's urban areas. It was the height of the crack cocaine epidemic in the inner city (Boyd, *H.N.I.C.*; Floyd, *Power of Black Music;* George and National Urban League, *Stop the Violence*; Hodge, *Heaven Has a Ghetto;* Hassan, "Post-Modernism"; Kitwana, *Hip Hop Generation;* Oliver, "Streets"; Ruskin, *Hip Hop Project*).

5. Otis Moss, "Real Big." I use the term "ghetto" throughout the manuscript and that is done for several key reasons: 1) it symbolizes an impoverished, disenfranchised area outside of geographic constraints, given the depth and growth of gentrification in communities once known for being "inner-city" and/or "ghetto; 2) it is a term that was synonymous with Tupac and his language in referring to poor Black and Latinx communities. I felt it necessary to incorporate that language in this book as well.

and post-soul[6] resistance for decades to come.[7] Hip Hop was, and still is, a way to construct thought, question authority, and express anger, frustration, hate, revolutionary worldviews, and rebellious spirits.

Additionally, Hip Hop created a space for people like myself to find a way in life. My life, especially during the crack era of the 1980s, was increasingly filled with messages such as be a "good" student and "turn the other cheek," but in my school, there were White racist classmates who tried to beat me up every day during recess and after school. Doing well in school and getting good grades was difficult because my teachers lowered my grades unfairly. The idea that Blacks cannot score higher than their White peers was a reality. Thus, "doing good" meant surviving, often in a physical sense. So, Hip Hop created, and continues to create, a voice to push back on these types of double messages. It is a vehicle in which those who are questioning authority, challenging dominant narratives of normality, the disenfranchised, and voiceless, can still find solace in a community of other like-minded people. It is a space in which communities can yell and be angry while eliciting violent images through song and lyrical prose. Hip Hop is a basic connection to that which looks, feels, talks, smells,

6. This term is used to describe the period and era that followed the soul era. Both of these terms, originated by George, *Buppies, B-Boys, Baps & Bohos*, are contextualized for what postmodernism is for Black, Latino, Urban, and Hip Hop contexts and which includes such societal shifts as the civil rights movement, the migrant farmworkers' movement, and the Black power movement—to name a few—which helped shape postmodern elements of current societal mores. George, *Post-Soul Nation*; and Hodge, *Heaven Has a Ghetto*.

7. The civil unrest in Libya, Egypt, and Paris had Hip Hop as its core voice and used US artists such as KRS-One, The Roots, Tupac Shakur, Lauryn Hill, and N.W.A. (among many others) as templates for social revolutions.

laughs, cries, and moves, like you—the community of those living in oppressed or disenfranchised conditions.

Music, in its rawest form, is powerful. Ethnomusicologists Mark Slobin and Jeff Todd Titon contend that "every human society has music. Music is universal; but its meaning is not."[8] Therefore it is imperative that we study Hip Hop's musical meaning and expression in Rap to better understand its theological message. Music speaks, but the context in which it was created—the sociopolitical, the sociogeographical, the sociotheological, and the time period—speaks as the artist crafts music from within that space.[9] Thus, the context and culture in which music is born is a crucial part of its meaning, social nuance, rhythmic construction, and lyrical pathway. When music is able to transcend culture in a way that creates meaning for people, then there are aspects such as transcendental meaning, spiritual identity, and theological construction that are worth investigating. In other words, when you consider the societal and living conditions of urban enclaves within the United States, their history of development, the exclusion of Blacks from society for centuries, the ongoing issue of police brutality, and the rise of the prison industrial complex, it can be overwhelming and debilitating. Yet, Hip Hop culture does not back down. It delves into these issues while creating a space of identity and relevance for its listeners. One must foster an understanding of the cultural conditions, context, geographical location, political atmosphere, social events, cultural background, and theological conditions in which a Hip Hop artist chooses to write their song. This allows for a clearer and much more rigorous understanding of to whom and what the music is speaking.

8. Slobin and Titon, "Music-Culture as a World of Music," 1.

9. Costen, "Protest and Praise"; Spencer, *Theological Music*.

Music has always been about expressing time and space within a current context and current setting.[10] Music sets moods, creates atmospheres, and can transport you to another time and dimension. Its very rhythm can take you to the same place or taste that you experienced when you first heard that particular song. Music is just that powerful.

Therefore, it should be no surprise that Rap is such a powerful medium for so many people. As Murray Forman has noted, "Hip-hop has evolved into one of North America's most influential youth oriented forces. It provides a sustained articulation of the social partitioning of race and the diverse experiences of being young and black or Latino in North America."[11] When DJ Jazzy Jeff and The Fresh Prince won the first Rap Grammy in 1989, the entire music industry was changed and it marked the dawn of a new era for both Hip Hop and America. Hip Hop and Rap remain a powerful social and musical might in the shaping of American pop culture.

To ground us even further, here is a working definition of Hip Hop:

> Hip Hop is an urban sub-culture that seeks to express a life-style, attitude, and/or urban individuality. Hip Hop at its core—not the commercialization and commodity it has become in certain respects—rejects dominant forms of culture and society and seeks to increase a social consciousness along with a racial/ethnic pride. Thus, Hip Hop uses rap music, dance, music production, MCing, and allegory as vehicles to send and fund its message of social, cultural, and political resistance to dominate structures of norms.[12]

10. Spencer, *Theological Music*, 3–5.
11. Forman, *'Hood Comes First*, 3.
12. For a further examination of this definition see, Hodge, *Hip*

Note the parts of this definition that emphasize rejection of dominant forms of culture—messages of resistance to social, cultural, and political spaces. This is powerful. This is part of what Glover, for example, is after. Therefore, Hip Hop is a central theme throughout the "This Is America" video. To prove this point even further, Kendrick Lamar, the quintessential post-soul Hip Hop theologian,[13] is able to surpass the commercialized arena of Rap music while creating locality for young Blacks to question norms, disrupt hegemonic mores, and find solace in their own personal development. Laced with tracks that speak from the definition of Hip Hop culture, Lamar challenges minds to think about resistance.

Rap music, conversely, is defined as such:[14]

> Rap is the main medium of the Hip-Hop culture that brings definition, value, understanding, and appreciation to the social isolation, economic hardship, political demoralization and cultural exploitation endured by most ghetto & poor White communities.
>
> Thus, rap is the musical expression that compliments the oral communication of its culture. Rap also captures and esteems the ghetto poor existence as valid and real to all people of color, including many poor Whites. Rap brings the revenue, which fuels the culture and its message.[15]

Here, we have a more hermeneutical discourse of the culture: the voice, the message, the audience, the transmediated composition of what rappers do and how they

Hop's Hostile Gospel.

13. Hodge, *Hip Hop's Hostile Gospel*, 57–90.

14. Parts of this definition are also adapted from Smith and Jackson, *Hip Hop Church.*

15. Hodge, *Heaven Has a Ghetto,* 69.

do it. The expression of rappers, in their original premise for the culture, was to: 1) create a type of unity through community involvement; 2) develop an awareness of the arts through the utilization of contextualized instruments (e.g., the turntable, the mouth through beat-boxing); and 3) esteem a povertized existence as a valid way of life and that being "poor" was not a bad thing—a strong message for those living under the scrutiny of the Reagan '80s.[16] Rap would be the undergirding of Hip Hop culture, yet notice the latter part of the definition, the revenue. Anytime money gets involved, especially in large amounts, the soul is in jeopardy of being lost. Yet, as Glover has recently showed us, Hip Hop and Rap are not dead.

Figure 1 below shows us the core of Hip Hop's culture:

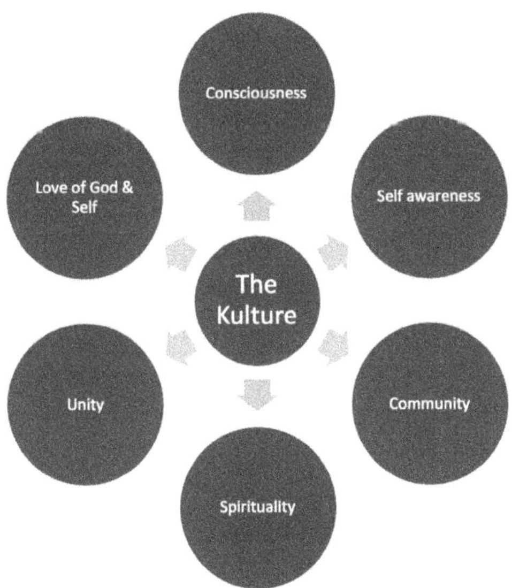

Figure 1: Core Principals of Hip Hop Culture

16. Check out Chang, *Can't Stop Won't Stop*; Dyson, *Between God and Gangsta Rap*; George, *Hiphop America*; George, *Post-Soul Nation*; Hodge, *Heaven Has a Ghetto*; Hodge, "No Church in the Wild."

Here we see a much broader view of Hip Hop that goes beyond those commercial restraints that so many power 100 stations put it in. This is a much stronger view of how Tupac was formed and the mechanics of what he was after: consciousness, community, spirituality, and a love of God and self. These are important elements, that, if we had the time, we could take back to fifth century middle Africa. Hip Hop is not disconnected from the African experience prior to colonizers emerging on its shores. Thus, Hip Hop is still attempting to establish those roots. In other words, Hip Hop is a contextualized postmodern approach to oppression using the medium afforded to it, music/video, and thereby creating the veneration of Black and Latinx bodies as valid and real; as Tupac would say, "Just because a person poor, don't mean they is bad or a robber. They're just poor and in need of help."

Hip Hop and the Post-Soul

Studies in postmodernism, largely, just leave out PoCs. It's like we don't exist. So, as in Hip Hop, we—meaning PoC—must create our own space. Scholars such as Mark Anthony Neal, Michael Eric Dyson, and Nelson George use a more contextual term for what has come to be known as postmodernism: that term is post-soul. Post-soul is a rejection of soul era values, traditions, metanarratives, theological accounts, and societal structures stemming from hierarchal systems attempting to control various societal areas—you can see why Hip Hop is such a strong component in the post-soul. Nelson George tells us, "Documenting the post-soul era is not about chronicling the straight line of a social movement, but collecting disparate fragments that form not a linear story, but a collage."[17] Further, the post-soul vernacular better suits the Black and Brown social structure. Mark Anthony Neal says, "The political, social, and cultural expressions of the African-American community since the civil rights and Black power movements" is essentially the point of birth for the post-soul era.[18] Neal notes that these persons born and/or raised during this era came to age during the tumultuous 1980s and were first-hand witnesses to Reaganomics, with its destructive forces in the 'hood. They experienced change from industrialism to deindustrialization, witnessed segregation to desegregation, went from strong clear notions of Blackness to nostalgic and metanarratives on Blackness, and even within these parameters of potential despair were still firmly in grasp of existential concerns within Black and Brown communities.[19]

Therefore, the term post-soul and its era is one that encompasses the aforementioned, but also embraces the significance of race, class, and gender within its scope of ideology. Post-soul is the cradle in which Hip Hop is able to create its theological and spiritual sensibilities and the nebula in which Tupac was able to do what he did. This period and shift from the soul era took full figuration during the mid to late 1960s[20] and it is there that we begin our discussion on the soul and post-soul development.

17. George, *Post-Soul Nation*, ix.

18. Neal, *Soul Babies*, 3.

19. Neal also contends that the post-soul era could be feasibly documented in its emergence with the rise of the 1980s "Reagan Right." It is because of this, Neal argues, that Reagan's policies further helped to instigate the advent of Hip Hop music and culture as Hip Hop became the most visible site of an already hostile and oppositional urban youth culture. Neal, *Soul Babies*, 102–03.

20. I argue that during this particular period, a shift and turn away

Soul and Post-Soul/Post-civil Rights Context Variations

The post-soul era is better understood by first understanding what the soul era was. The soul era arguably begins with the end of World War II. It had several key elements to it that ring true and authentic to many who lived through some of the events that shaped it. Those key elements are:

- Connection to the faith community.
- The soul culture that produced Marvin Gaye, Aretha Franklin, Jackie Wilson, Sam Cooke, and Donnie Hathaway.
- It brought its religion's worldviews to the marketplace and public sphere.
- It was nurtured in the womb of church, religious settings, and pastor-centered theologies.
- They had optimism on their side and wanted to work with certain power structures to affect change.

Faith and religious overtones mark the norms, values, and belief system of the soul era, especially in the Black Christian church. The soul era embraced an American Dream-type of social element that many strived to achieve, and also produced a sense of morality rooted deeply in a King James Version of God.[21] It was a time in which the

from traditional modes of thought within Black traditions began to form. It began with Blacks standing up for their rights and refusing to conform to the social norms of White American society. Further, it was a time when some Blacks felt the power to speak up against Jim and Jane Crowism and the injustice that had befallen them for too long. It is also the era in which Hip Hop is, in essence, groomed and made ready for the coming storm of the 1980s.

21. To put this another way, a very rigid, fundamental, and binary view (sin vs. salvation) of theology and life.

equation of life issues was A + B = C; binary; good vs. evil; things were, for White hetero families, clear and not "complicated." In other words, life had answers and "clear paths" were evident eventually. Wouldn't that be nice?

Theologically, patriarchal respect and reverence characterized the soul era when it was uncommon for young people to question the authority of older men. Further, Black Christian churches were, in principle, a social structure for the creation of meaning, social representations of God, and spaces in which answers to life were eventually "found."

The soul era took the values of post–World War II Black life and embraced it to its fullest. A "soulist" found themselves in a world that made sense, in one regard, and even though racism, segregation, and lynching were horrendous acts, life was still "black and white." The suburbanization and rise of American pop culture during the 1950s aided in creating a national social ethos in which life appeared to be "simpler" and "neater." *Father Knows Best*, *Leave It to Beaver*, and *Bewitched*, to name just a few of the growing television series of the time, made life seem compacted into a simple thirty-minute fix. For the soulist, this made sense and helped to create a place for life, even if it was at the back of a bus.

In the soul era, the "enemy" was clear: White racism, segregation, and inequality. The civil rights generation (1945–70) were united against these clear enemies who threatened to destroy the very fabric of Black and Brown life. The leaders of this time, Cesar Chavez, Martin Luther King Jr., Malcolm X, John Brown, Linda Brown, Ruby Bridges, and Medgar Evers, were clear in their operative: destroy these enemies and create a "better tomorrow." The soul era still had clear leadership, despite the declining financial status of many Black Americans, and this leadership had the ability to unify groups and masses.

The soul era inherited the struggles of previous generations of Blacks and urban poor who were united by several social and collective problems: struggle, pursuit of democracy, fighting the oppressive hegemony, justice movements, and a common working knowledge of God, typically rooted in Christianity. These social and collective adhesives were passed down, generationally speaking, and they galvanized young people around singularized leaders (e.g., King, Chavez) who "spoke for all" in the public sphere. This also created a sense of community among oppressed peoples, be they Latinx, Black, or even women. The soul era had the public personalities to engage with, to learn from, and to embrace on many levels.[22]

The post-soul era, by contrast, lost most of those leaders who were formidable and connected to the ghetto community. Further, within the post-soul era the "enemy" became muddled and unclear: was it the Vietnamese, classism, White people, or the FBI? To add an even stranger phenomenon, when segregation ended, what once was a thriving section of Black households and communities now became split. If a family had some aspect of economic refuge, they were more than likely to move out of the "ghetto" and into better neighborhoods, especially now that segregation had ended. While I do not contend that

22. It can, therefore, be argued that, because of the loss of generational connectedness, social upheaval, and loss of historical connectivity during the late '60s and transition into the postmodern/post-soul era, the previous generation, which would become the first Hip Hop generation, was formed and created in a womb of dislocation, disenfranchisement, and a cultural anomie in which life was seen as misguided and with ambiguous direction. In this sense, the music and culture would in fact have much to say, both verbally and non-verbally, about these conditions.

we need to return to a segregated world, one of the side effects of integration was the splintering of Black social classes and the separation of Black elites and lower-class Blacks.[23] The post-soul era began in the late 1960s just as Black families were losing fathers and Black elites were moving out to the suburbs.[24]

Hence, one of the crucial differences between the soul and post-soul era was its connection to previous generations and historical narratives for life, community, and personal vision. This predominantly affected Black families. From 1965–71, Black low-income communities were run by community groups such as the Student Nonviolent Coordinating Committee, the NAACP, and the Black Panther Party. There was a sense of social consciousness and awareness among the youth, and the old and young were still working side by side. The young were still attaining the knowledge from the preceding generations. These community organizations were committed to seeing change from within the Black community and from within the self—self-knowledge and self-awareness. Kumasi Brown, a South Los Angeles social activist and community historian, tells us about this time: "all them

---

23. A phenomenon Michael Eric Dyson describes as the Ghettoistocracy and the Afristocracy of Black classes. Dyson, *Is Bill Cosby Right?*

24. Even social unrest was shifting during this time. Prior to the 1960s, rioting was typically Whites marauding through Black neighborhoods instilling on them violence in some shape or form, but the riots of the mid 1960s in Detroit, Oakland, and Los Angeles were Blacks revolting against the historical forms of injustice and racism in this country. From that point forward, "rioting" would not be the same, and most riots were in protest and rejection of "American" standards that many Black and Brown families living in the ghetto rejected and saw as a form of oppression (Sides, *L.A. City Limit;*, Peralta, *Crips and Bloods*, Wiese, *Places of Their Own*).

youngsters were busy trying to rebuild their communities, trying to rebuild their futures, trying to figure out where the fuck do we go from here . . . together. And how do we create some sense of a future for our people?"[25] However, these community organizations, like the Black Panthers, quickly found themselves in the crosshairs of government organizations like the FBI. According to recently declassified papers, the Black Panther Party was under constant observation, was deemed a "threat to national security," and was quickly labeled as both a "terrorist organization" and an "extremist group" that "advocated violence against American citizens."[26] These documents also reveal the fear and continual attempts, eventually ending in success, to destroy such community groups because of their "un-American" stance toward nationalism. To further this, almost anyone connected to such parties would be automatically followed, spied on, and deemed "hostile."[27] J. Edgar Hoover described organizations like the Panthers as "the greatest threat to the internal security of America."[28] Kumasi once again firmly asserts, "they [the US government] turned around and squashed those movements," and some of the greatest and most energetic leaders of

25. Taken from an interview with Mr. Brown in September 2010.

26. Taken from article 33 of 34 in the FBI vault files. http://vault.fbi.gov/Black%20Panther%20Party%20/Black%20Panther%20Party%20Part%2033%20of%2034/view.

27. This was the case for two African American soldiers who showed interest in Black community development; they were followed and their activities were monitored. http://vault.fbi.gov/Black%20Panther%20Party%20/Black%20Panther%20Party%20Part%2033%20of%2034/view.

28. Taken from an interview Hoover did with *TIME* magazine on December 14, 1970. "Nation: J. Edgar Hoover Speaks Out With Vigor." http://content.time.com/time/magazine/article/0,9171,944193,00.html.

that time were either murdered, sent to prison, or fled the country in exile. Within a few years, between 1965–70, many of the iconic leaders within the Black community were no longer there and a colossal void began settling in for Blacks. By 1971, there were very few remaining voices for Black youth to look toward, ghettos continued to swell, and Black Americans began a quick descent into extreme poverty, gang violence, and disenfranchisement.[29]

The youth born during this time were disconnected and disjointed from society—keep in mind Tupac was born June 16, 1971. Moreover, with the rise in the absence of Black fathers during this time, Black youth found it difficult to adjust in a world that was not socially logical to them. Mr. Brown once again states, "We passed by these children every day and paid no attention to them because we figured they'd be eventually taken care of. But, they watched us. We had the generations our parents came from and we had the personalities from that generation to connect with! To inspire us! We had something to attach ourselves to. They [the youth during this period] did not. They [the youth] were born in a state of suspended animation; they were totally disconnected and disenfranchised. They're like a planet out of orbit!"[30]

Therefore, it should stand to reason that the post-soul era was not formed in the womb of the church as the soul era was. The post-soulist did not have the connections to a "faith" community as did the soulists. Hip Hoppers,

29. It is also interesting to note that at the same time these leaders were being extinguished in Black communities, the rise of the two infamous gangs, the Crips and the Bloods, grew exponentially (Peralta 2008; Sides 2003). I recommend reading Jeff Chang's chapter on the gangs of the Bronx ("Can't Stop Won't Stop") as he also makes these connections.

30. Taken from an interview with Mr. Brown in September 2010.

who are mainly the offspring of those from the post-soul era, had to develop their sense of being, their sense of life, their identity, and their values outside the church environment and, as Otis Moss states, "It nursed from the breast of market forces and morally ambiguous political ideology."[31] Moreover, the post-soul offspring strongly critique the status quo and institutions. Hip Hop is no different, which is one of the many reasons it has a difficult time finding solace in "church." The post-soul era was born during a time of deep urban difficulties and speaks for not just Hip Hoppers and Blacks, but also Latinos, poor ghettoized Whites, and disenfranchised Asians. Otis Moss once again states:

> The truth is that many people of color, especially youth, are fighting for survival and attempting to gather meaning out of this strange land called America. With the increase of police repression, demonization of people of color, introduction of crack cocaine, and the de-industrialization of urban centers, black people find themselves at a crossroads. Old tactics and strategies of change are now obsolete.[32]

Paul Taylor, in his article "Post Black, Old Black" stresses that within the post-soul era, "new meanings have emerged: new forms of black identity that are multiple, fluid, and profoundly contingent, along with newly sophisticated understandings of race and identity,"[33] marking what Mark Anthony Neal contends as the "shift from essential notions of blackness to metanarratives on blackness" within the post-soul milieu.[34] Additionally, post-soul

31. Moss, "Real Big," 11.

32. Chang, *Can't Stop Won't Stop*, 113.

33. Taylor, "Post-Black, Old Black," 626.

34. Neal, *Soul Babies*, 3.

Hip Hoppers largely find solace in an image that Todd Boyd describes as "The Nigga"—a rebellious, outspoken, system-rejecting, and irreverent yet proud and socially focused image of Black aesthetics, which revels in questioning, authoring, and recovering some of those broken promises, often by any means necessary,[35] which is what Tupac talked about in many of his interviews. Thus, within the post-soul era, Hip Hop finds itself in a Marxist state of mind as it critiques the socioeconomics, social climate, and institutions of America.

Table 1 below has a brief way of better understanding some significant components between the soul era and the post-soul era:

Table 1: The Differences Between the Soul Era and the Post-Soul Era

Soul Era	Post-Soul Era
Was and still is Absolute; right and wrong are clear	Non-absolute, majority thinking; institutions create evil policy and wrong is rooted in that
Linear in reasoning and leadership; there is always someone "at the top" within institutions	Non-linear; circular, triangular, and extremely visual, and leadership is localized; think of Black Lives Matter chapters, there is no singular leader, only local community leaders
Hierarchal; top-down power; order to power structures; men, typically, lead, you can allow some women, but men have the last word	Group-centered and power is equally distributed and plural; women take on a much stronger focus here and create disruption to male dominance

35. Boyd, *Am I Black Enough for You?*, 13–37. This image and characterization of Hip Hop only reinforces the notion that Hip Hop is hostile, secular, devoid of God, and immoral for those who reside in soul-era worldviews.

Individualists; individualism is valued; "it's your fault" if it's that way, not the system	Community-based while still allowing for individual creativity and expression; systems and intuitions are key in shaping how people decide how to behave and engage
Logic toward solutions and answers; work for solutions and practice a method to arrive there	Logic gets thrown to the side in the face of oppression; logic is developing and if the method hasn't worked, it's time for something new
Solid conclusions every time; there are answers	Ambiguity; life is a mystery; answers can be lies and another form of oppression
Answers that are solid and conclusive; everything can be explained in life; the hermeneutic are sacred texts be it political, theological, or otherwise	Uncertainty; everything does not have to have an answer; one must continue to search for their own truth and deconstruct the colonized mind
Race is in the binary (Black and White); race is what matters; gender and sexual orientation are footnotes	Race is complex and mixed in with ethnicity; intersectionality is key; you cannot talk about racial oppression without engaging gender oppression
Categorizing people, places, and things; everything has its place	Every person, place, and thing cannot be categorized and explained; there are people, places, and things that simply cannot be explained
Godhead is set; theology is clear	God is plural, existential, and mystical; theological pursuits are ongoing; for some, religion is oppressive and must be avoided at all costs

These areas are by no means exhaustive. Yet they give us a place in which to begin and to better understand why Hip Hop helps to usher in post-soul tendencies and, more importantly, what formed Tupac's ideological structure. Moreover, Hip Hop begins new didactic conversations in regard to Christology, salvation, and kingdom of God discourse. Just look at Kendrick's album, *Damn*, for an example.

Thus, for the post-soulist, life is unpredictable, mysterious, questionable. Systems will fail you and eventually, almost everyone will lie to you. When we contrast that with the soul era, we see a stark difference in attitudinal values toward life. Moreover, the two are almost at odds on issues of faith, God, and especially "church."[36] When this is put into context, we can now think about a post-civil rights era and generation.

The post-civil rights context/era is the generation of youth born during the post-soul era/context, raised on a transmediated diet, disconnected from previous generations both locally and ideologically, and currently have non-binary issues to contend with in a post-9/11 Western society. This generation of young people do not

36. It is important to note that Rap groups such as Public Enemy and NWA gave voice and breath to Hip Hop's post-soul aesthetic. These two groups were strongly criticized for their stance and critique on many social problems that existed and still exist today in the US. They also put a face on much of Rap music that still exists today. The "ugly" side of post-soul is the commercialization and the pervasive and negative messages it sends to all people of color living in America. Public Enemy and NWA represented social critiques, yet ironically enough, their critique was lost within the commercialization of the post-soul era while their "style" still remains. Many who do not have a grasp on Hip Hop culture or who have never been to an inner city, see Hip Hop largely looking like these two groups: Black, exotic yet ominous, dark, and having an "in your face" attitude. This concept has brought billions of dollars to many corporations and has made large sections of the Black community a laughing stock and the butt of many jokes. The post-soul era's commercialization has made it "okay" to Niggarize the suburbs; films such as Whitesell, *Malibu's Most Wanted*, are an example of this.

have the binary issues to contend with that the civil rights generation did (e.g., more Blacks in leadership or the right to vote). While those issues are still present, they manifest themselves in a matrix of problems, which involve sexuality, sexual orientation, socioeconomics, transgenderism, class, and race. This is the era and context of Tupac. This era and context is what is typically referred to as the boomer generation (1948–69) but the civil rights generation terminology encompasses a much broader multiethnic variable and it would include those born between 1945 and 1970. This era is stooped in the church and raised on traditional primarily Protestant Christian values. This era saw the likes of Marvin Gaye, Aretha Franklin, and Ray Charles. Culturally speaking, there was a linear process to "life" and society. The soul era is etched with faith and religious overtones that mark its norms, values, and belief system strongly in the Christian church—especially the Black Christian church. The soul era embraced an American Dream type of social element in which many strived to achieve.[37] Leadership was top down and singularized—meaning one voice for the masses. It was a period that helped shape a large part of the African American diaspora in the US. It also situated the Black Church as the authority and sociopolitical space for justice and civil protests. Without this period, there would be no Hip Hop, soul, funk, disco, or Black liberation movement.

Still, even with the optimism of Black middle-class life during the 1950s and the great hope of the civil-rights movement of the 1960s, the post-soul context/era came at a time when Black values in the public sphere were declining and leaders of Black life, iconic even in their own

37. See Hodge, *Hip Hop's Hostile Gospel*, chapter 1; Hodge, *Soul of Hip Hop*, chapter 2.

time, were either killed or sent off into exile; the following generation was then raised in that void and in a time when media was creating tropes of Black life in shows like *The Jeffersons* (1975–85) and *Sanford and Son* (1972–77). This is the era and context following the soul era and similar to what is termed the postmodern period. The post-soul context/era lost its leadership and this emerging generation, those born from 1971 on, was disconnected from earlier ones. The youth born during this time were disconnected and disjointed from society. Moreover, with the rise in the absence of Black fathers during this time,[38] Black youth, especially, found it difficult to adjust in a world that was not socially, religiously, and morally logical to them and without the guidance of caring adults. This era created the first Hip Hop generation.

Hip Hop and Postmodernism

Okay, I get it, this may sound hypocritical in title. I get that. But I find it is necessary to have a brief discussion of Hip Hop and its relation to postmodernism. I realize that the term "postmodernism" has become quite stale and what was once a buzz word in the 1990s is now growing old. While I am not presenting an exhaustive study regarding this very important relationship, there are works such as Cornel West's *Prophetic Thought in Postmodern Times* and Lawrence Cahoone's *From Modernism to Postmodernism*, which treat this extensively. It does, however, deserve some discussion at the very least in relation to Hip Hop.

38. Hattery and Smith, *African American Families*, 9–37. There is a host of literature discussing the denigration of Black fathers and the creation of the welfare system during the late 1960s and early 1970s.

Hip Hop, during the 1980s and 1990s, set the stage for public voices and a new form of music.[39] Russell Potter says that Hip Hop and Rap were one of the leading agents for postmodernism to develop in regards to language; it was the music and language for the postmodern generation.[40] The music became the philosophical base for Hip Hop artists. In modernity, modern social theory sought a universal, historical, and rational foundation for its analysis and critique of society. For postmodernists, there is a rejection of that "universal" thought and message. Postmodern thinking rejects this "foundationalism" and tends to be relativistic, irrational, and nihilistic. Postmodernists have come to question foundations structured within systems and institutions, believing that they tend to favor some groups and downgrade the significance of others, give some groups power, and render other groups powerless.[41]

Cornel West[42] also adds three significant changes in American culture that gave rise to postmodernism in the US. West offers a genealogy of how this moment in time, postmodernity, came about.[43]

The first is the displacement of European models of high culture, of Europe as the universal subject of culture,

39. Another reason Rap music is so appealing to contemporary generations is because, through postmodernism, one can express her or his self in a unique way and find a voice within that music. See Alper, "Making Sense"; Anderson ("Black Beats"), and Forman (*'Hood Comes First*).

40. Potter, *Spectacular Vernaculars.*

41. See White, "Constructions of Identity," 200; Hall discusses this cultural change in which Black popular culture developed in his "What Is This 'Black,'" 21–25.

42. West, "New Cultural Politics," 32–33.

43. These three points are adapted from West, "New Cultural Politics," 19–36.

and of culture itself in its old Arnoldian reading as the last "refuge." In this sense, the Eurocentric school of thought in many ways made Blacks invisible and nameless. Within a Eurocentric hegemony there is a lack of Black power in the social sphere. Yet, with the emergence of popular culture, forms of art such as rock and roll, jazz, and the blues, became vehicles in which Blacks gained voice and some power, relatively speaking, while shifting the Eurocentric authority and giving space for a new form of thought.

The second coordinate that West discusses is the emergence of the United States as a world power, through the means of slavery and the rise of capitalism during the nineteenth century. Consequently, the US became the center of global and cultural production and circulation. This made it possible for America to grow economically and socioeconomically. John Hall says that "this emergence is both a displacement and a hegemonic shift in the definition of culture—a movement from high culture to American mainstream popular culture and its mass-cultural, image mediated, technological forms."[44]

The third area that West describes is the decolonization of the third world, culturally marked by the emergence of the decolonized sensibilities.[45] The world was becoming gradually autotomized. America was developing what we now refer to as popular culture and the rise of the inner city, of the ghetto, was developing as previously mentioned. The inner city was therefore set up to be a cultural hub. Nonetheless, the industrial revolution played a large role as urban areas grew, decolonization happened globally, and Black popular culture, which reflected the effects

44. Hall, "Capitals of Cultures," 21–22.

45. West, *Prophetic Thought in Postmodern Times*, 122–23.

of the industrial revolution, grew in American popular culture.[46]

Consequently, the postmodern context has origins in pop culture and the media. The postmodern context has two very distinct characteristics. First, it is spiritual. I know, I know, this is an arguable point to make. Intellectuals such as Zygmunt Bauman, Don Cupitt, and Martin Heidegger would contend that postmodernism rejects modern spirituality and religion and begins on a quest toward some form of secularization.[47] Charles Taylor would even assert that we do in fact live in a "secular age" with the advent of postmodernity.[48] Yet, while these scholars have valid points, the postmodern (particularly the post-soul era) is still in search of a God, spirituality, and faith; it merely looks, acts, feels, and walks very differently than anything in modernity. Second, postmodernity presents a consciousness of pluralism on every level of social engagement. In other words, the postmodern age is a re-enchantment of the "forest" of life, society, the human experience, theology, spirituality, and faith. For the postmodernist, the "forest" is not managed, predicted, and produced away; the "forest" is a mystery. Moreover, for Hip Hoppers, the "forest" cannot be controlled by White managers who continue to dictate what is "right" and "wrong." Hip Hop, then, calls out that mismanagement and proclaims the "forest" to be a fluid object that cannot be manufactured in cookie-cutter ways; Tupac is about engaging in this re-enchantment.

46. Also see Cone, *Black Theology and Black Power*, on how the rise of the "suffering Jesus" came into play and how that played out in Black culture and the urban gospel message (chapter 6).

47. Bauman, "Postmodern Religion?"; Cupitt, "Post-Christianity"; and Heidegger, "Letter on Humanism."

48. Taylor, "Post-Black, Old Black."

The focus is on the spectacular,[49] on the edge, and on allowing the person to reach a higher level of knowledge. Any culture that focuses on the spectacular might be termed a transcendent culture. Life is over the top; the unreal is the real. Postmodernists are searching for the experiential and the transcendence in culture, which includes Rap music.

Okay, whew! I know that was a lot, and if you can believe it, this is just scratching the surface. That said, I think this is now setting us up for the rest of the book, which will focus exclusively on Tupac. What I've done here is given the context in which Tupac created his work; we now have something we can refer to when Pac talks about resisting conventional religion and questioning authority at all costs. Let's now take a closer look into the eras of Tupac's life and what shaped each one.

49. Graffiti art is one of the most powerful aesthetic expressions of postmodern Hip Hop discourse. This is very similar to what Emma Cavazzini argues in neo-avant-garde art in the postmodern global context (*Art of the 20th Century*).

2

Tupac's Life Eras and Sociotheological Spaces

It was a rare sunny day in the Bay Area in June. We had just finished up a Young Life Club and the kids I was working with were coming out of the Boys & Girls Club. One young brother got in the passenger seat of the van and popped in a cassette tape into the deck—yes, that was the way we listened to music in the old days. It was Tupac's latest album, *Me Against the World*. This brother wanted me to play the tape because it was such a strong album and he felt that Tupac was talking about Jesus and pain. I looked at him as if he had asked to marry my sister, of which I have no sibling. Can you imagine, a secular artist filled with vulgarity and profanity, playing in the church van? Oh hell naw! Thus ensued what would become known as the "showdown talk" for ages to come. See, I was quite the fundamentalist then. I subscribed to a strict Seventh Day Adventist theology, which saw the world in binary terms: evil and good were clear; God was on one side, the devil on the other; life made sense. Artists like Tupac messed that up. I can't believe I fought with those students of mine for so long regarding Tupac. That wasn't the last time we had a showdown talk either. I have since attempted to find that cohort of youth and apologize to them. I was wrong, and they were right. Religion and the need to be right blinds us. Years later I would see exactly what they were trying to get me to see in Tupac. It just took some time, some pain and suffering of my own, and a complete worldview change. Man, that was a trip. It gave me a newfound respect for Tupac and I began asking the question, "how did someone like Tupac get as far as he did by age twenty-five? I wondered that for a long time. What shaped Tupac? How did his life begin and end? What did I miss when he was alive and making albums?

This chapter takes a closer look at the eras within Tupac's life. In my research I've used a method called ethno-lifehistory, which documents a person's life beyond just a biography, but examines the shaping moments throughout their life: the good, the bad, the ugly, and everything in between. What I've done is broken down Tupac's life into five major life eras. This will help us both digest his amazing life better and understand the shaping factors of his music and thought process. So, with that, let's get in it.

Military Mind (1971–80)

Where did it all begin? On June 16, 1971, in the Bronx, New York, Lesane Parish Crooks was born to Afeni Shakur. Tupac's original name was Lesane Parish Crooks, but Afeni later changed his name to Tupac Amaru Shakur. The name was derived from an Incan Chief who was torn apart by Spaniards, meaning, "Shining serpent, thankful to God."[1] Afeni had been involved in the Black Panther movement for quite some time. Tupac's father remains a bit of a mystery. William Garland is thought to be his biological father,

1. Peters, *Tupac Vs.*

while Jeral Williams, a.k.a. Dr. Mutulu Shakur, is his stepfather and mentor.

Afeni was a revolutionary. She had been actively involved with the Black Panther movement and vigorously stood for their principles and platform.[2] Afeni threw herself into the Panther 21 (their name at the time) in 1968. She attended rallies, gave speeches, and protested the racist attitude of American White culture of the time. In 1969, she was arrested for allegedly trying to bomb several buildings in Manhattan, New York. In February of 1971, she was sent to the Women's Detention Center in Greenwich Village where in June of that same year, Tupac was born. To his own admission, he was cultivated in prison. Tupac said, "My mom was pregnant with me in prison, and after she got out (a month before her due date) she gave birth to me. I was cultivated in prison; my embryo was made in prison."

Being pregnant with Tupac in prison, Afeni helped to shape some of the love and hate that many urban youth deal with in regards to prison. Tupac did not want to go to jail, but it gave him more street credibility—more on this in his outlaw era.

Afeni defended herself in court, and through hard work, persistence, and her knowledge of the law, she was found not guilty of attempting to bomb a government building. She was free to go. This set a precedent for Tupac that lasted his whole life: never give up!

The Black Panther Party

The Black Panther Party's vision of Black unity, Black power, Black independence, and self-sustaining power

2. See Attachment C for a copy of the Black Panther's ten-point platform and program.

was an intricate part of Afeni's life. This in turn transferred directly into Tupac's life.

The Black Panther Party was about helping Black people. They adopted the message of civil rights and equal rights, spoken of by Martin Luther King Jr., which stated that we are no longer taking the "crap" we took in the 1960s; we are no longer taking the dysfunction that America calls racism; we are no longer capitulating, no longer surrendering to the will of White America; we are standing up for ourselves and we have a platform to do that. It was a return to the Blackness of the soul, and a building up of Black people. This was a theme in the 1970s.[3]

The Black Panther Party educated themselves and began to understand the law of the land. They knew the law and understood how to interact with it and deal with it. Afeni was a large part of that faction. She was an avid reader and a devoted student of the law. Armond White states:

> Although the seventies had been relatively complacent, Black America found itself confronting new social challenges that threatened to reignite the activism and rage that had exploded in the sixties. Young Tupac's dream of revolution stood out—a rare raised fist amongst the millions of kiddie hands clutching Pac-Man joysticks. His answer to Rev. Daughtry reflects Afeni's experience and her soberly-adjusted attitude toward social change—his mothers son's loyalty mixed with an early sense of inherited mission.[4]

3. As also seen in many of the films and songs of that time. *Superfly*, *Shaft*, and *Foxy Brown* are just a few of the many Black pride films of the 1970s.

4. White, *Rebel for the Hell of It*, 3.

Tupac was raised with the mentality of helping each one and reaching each one. For many Blacks during this era, this too was their mantra. In an early interview, Tupac said, "My mother always taught me that if I wasn't doing or living for Black people, what was I living for?" The Black Panther Party stood for helping the next generation, the young people. Afeni embraced this idea, especially after Tupac was born.

Afeni instilled a sense of civil duty for Blacks, particularly ghetto Blacks, in Tupac. The Black Panther Party wanted to help end ghetto poverty and build up the communities that were torn down. Tupac's response to Reverend Daughtry's question of life goals was, "I want to be a revolutionary!"[5] This statement was at age ten.

Tupac, even at age five and eight, was continually trying to help out young Blacks. Even in church, he would want to be a part of the marches and speeches that helped the community he lived in. By age nine, he had memorized the Panther's ten point platform and program and desired to put those issues to use in the Black community.

Tupac was raised to believe that he was a soldier bred to fight a war. This is seen early in some of his lyrics:

> As real as it seems the American Dream
> Ain't nothing but another calculated scheme
> To get us locked up shot up back in chains
> To deny us of the future rob our names
> Kept my history of mystery but now I see
> The American Dream wasn't meant for me.[6]

The reality was that Tupac had both revolutionary and thug in him.

5. White, *Rebel for the Hell of It*, 4.

6. Taken from Shakur, "Panther Power," *The Lost Tapes*, http://www.ohhla.com/YFA_2pac.html.

Tupac was partly raised by men in the streets considered by many to be pimps, hustlers, junkies, and common criminals. These are some of the minds that influenced him in his early work. The streets were his classroom and he was an A student, but not just in the violence and crime that occurs on the streets, but in how to overcome those issues. Tupac states:

> My father was a panther. I never knew where my father was or who my father was for sure. The times that I came up, was the late sixties. They were still having free love, they was just hittin' what they was hittin'. My mother wasn't married, and she got pregnant and had me, and I didn't have a father.
>
> My stepfather was a gangsta. A straight up street hustler. He loved the fact that the Panthers would go to jail and wouldn't snitch. He didn't even care my moms had a kid. He was like, "Oh, that's my son." Took care of me, gave me money, but he was like a criminal too. He was a drug dealer out there doing his thing—he only came, brought me money, and then left. I hate saying this cuz white people love hearing black people talking about this. But I know for a fact that had I had a father, I'd have some discipline, I'd have more confidence.[7]

Here we see that Tupac was beginning to make distinctions of who was real and who was there for him. Even at a very young age, Tupac had a keen sense about people and wisdom beyond his years.

Throughout this era in Tupac's life, we begin to see the makings of a Hip Hop revolutionary.[8] Throughout Tu-

7. Shakur et al., *Tupac: Resurrection.*

8. Part of that revolutionary came out in *Thug Life*, which focuses

pac's career, almost all would agree that Tupac was still a Black Panther in Hip Hop clothing. All of his music related back to the struggle of ghetto Blacks in one way or another. This era helped to solidify Tupac's hard-core, dedicated, devoted, and enthusiastic vigor for life, the urban community, urban youth, and Black people in general. The Black Panther connection through Afeni and extended family members helped shape Tupac's social awareness and construct his social identity.

More importantly, the Black Panther Party laid out a social norm that stayed with Tupac for the rest of his life. This belief system—which consisted of being respectful, being unified, having and earning trust and honor, and having a deep social awareness—was manifested in such songs as "Young Black Male," "Brenda's Got a Baby," "Strugglin," and "Black Jesuz," which have inspired many current Hip Hoppers such as Kanye West, The Game, Mike Jones, and Eminem.

Afeni

Throughout Tupac's early childhood years, Afeni was the centerpiece of his life. She instructed him on his life path. Moreover, her values, philosophy, ideology, and principles were transferred to him orally and through her actions. Tupac states, "My mom was my homie, we went through our stages . . . really all males period, but males from that ghetto mentality especially, have a deep love for their mamas cuzz they usually raise us by themselves."[9] Afeni had endured many hardships and was aware of difficult times.

---

in on helping the thugs, pimps, and people society has looked upon as "trash."

9. From Peters, *Tupac Vs.*

Afeni, through her experience, raised Tupac and gave him one of his first views of the world.

In the Black community, Mama is next to God. Mammas are the ones typically raising young men, predominantly young Black men. Grandmas and mammas are one and the same, and while most grandparents are enjoying their "years off from parenting," they are now doing "double duty" as they raise the second and third generations of children. Tupac, being raised by many women, began early in life to understand the complexities of womanhood and to appreciate and respect those complexities.[10] Tupac had many women around his life that helped him appreciate women and helped him better understand women as a whole; particularly Black women and women from the ghetto.

Afeni has always been a solid figure in Tupac's life; this is seen throughout his music and career. Afeni gave up the Black Panther movement to stay home with her children and raise them. Initially Afeni was still actively involved in the movement, but after several talks with her children, particularly Tupac, she decided to stay home and get a regular job to take care of her children. Tupac states about Afeni:

> My mother was a Black Panther and she was really involved in the movement. Just Black people bettering themselves and things like that. She

10. This is something that many do not know about Tupac. They hear the word "bitch" in one of his songs, and most will assume that he is refereeing to all women. For Pac, that is not the case. "Bitch" can be broken down into many aspects of womanhood. It can mean a tramp, someone who is a knucklehead, someone who is scared, and/or a woman who is a gold-digger and only dates men for their money. However, in most cases it is used negatively. For Tupac, though, he knew the differences between a woman and a bitch; within Hip Hop culture as a whole, there is a difference.

> was high in position in the party, which was unheard of because there was sexism, even in the Panthers. All my roots to the struggle are real deep.
>
> There's racism, so when the Panthers hit, the government panicked and they felt like the Panthers were detrimental to American society. So they raided every Panther's house, especially the ones who they felt like could do damage as an orator.[11]

Tupac discussed how he and Afeni went through their stages. They struggled to communicate since both of their personalities were so strong. Tupac was allowed to speak his mind, so long as he respected his mother. Respect was a fundamental issue for Tupac: respect infused with knowledge. Tupac states, "My mother, she's totally brilliant. Totally understanding and caring. And she's human—I mean, she'll be wrong a lot but we can talk about it. My mother taught me three things: respect, knowledge, and search for knowledge. It's an eternal journey."[12]

> Let knowledge drop
> Why should I be forced to play dumb?
> I know where I came from so I'm going to claim some
> But rocking to the top where the cream of the crop
> Suckers calling the cops but they can come and get dropped.[13]

In this early piece, we are able to see his construction of neopolitical Rap music. This was ahead of its time. For most Hip Hoppers in the late 1970s and early 1980s, the theme was about partying and having fun, while proving

11. Shakur et al., *Tupac: Resurrection.*

12. Shakur et al., *Tupac: Resurrection.*

13. Taken from Shakur, "Let Knowledge Drop," *The Lost Tapes*, http://www.ohhla.com/YFA_2pac.html.

to others you are the man and/or woman. For Tupac, however, this was certainly not the case. He saw a deplorable plaited theme in the different ghettos he lived in: poverty. Tupac hated poverty. He wanted to do something about it. Afeni instilled in him that he had the power to do so.

Afeni also knew that Tupac needed a man's role in his life. Tupac even states, "Your mother cannot calm you down the way a man can. Your mother can't reassure you the way a man can. My mother couldn't show me where my manhood was. You need a man to teach you how to be a man."[14] Afeni took Tupac to church. Reverend Daughtry was introduced to Tupac through Afeni while they lived in New York. At a young age Tupac was introduced to Christ and the Black church. He writes:

> God
>
> When I was alone and had nothing I asked 4 a friend 2 help me bear the pain no one came cxccpt . . . GOD
>
> When I needed a breath 2 rise from my sleep no one could help me except . . . GOD
>
> When all I saw was sadness and I needed answers no one heard me except . . . GOD
>
> So when I am asked who I give my unconditional love 2 look for no other name except . . . GOD.[15]

In this poem we begin to see the deep love that Tupac had for God. Tupac was affected by deep and complex issues at a very young age. For many young people, childhood years are filled with fun, games, trips to grandma's

14. Taken from an interview Tupac gave around 1995, interviewer unknown.

15. The poem "God" taken from: http://www.ohhla.com/anonymous/2_pac/the_rose/god.2pc.txt.

home in another state, or simply "being a kid." However, many inner city youth, like Tupac, deal with adult issues and are burdened with crime, murder, and violent acts; these years resemble those of a forty-five year old. Issues such as money, crime, jobs, and the welfare of the family are all areas Tupac had to deal with on a daily basis. Tupac states that when he was a kid, he remembers one moment of calm and peace, and three minutes after that, it was on! Afeni tried to shield him as much as she could, but poverty is a harsh reality and a kick in the ass. He saw death, sexual abuse, drugs, crime, violence, and hard-core life issues such as poverty and homelessness firsthand. Tupac had to face a reality that others were able to simply ignore. Afeni did her best to shield him from it, and to instill hope, but Tupac was introduced to the harsh realism of this world firsthand

Tupac hated poverty because he felt he and his family missed out on a lot. Afeni wanted to give her kids more, but could not. When Tupac did finally become a Rap superstar, he bought each of his family members houses, cars, and paid most of their bills.[16]

The Music and Arts

Tupac had an eclectic taste in music. Hip Hop culture during this time was in its early stages. Rap music could only be heard on underground mix tapes and at DJ parties. Rap groups such as Run DMC and LL Cool J were some of the more famous ones that made it onto the public scene. Hip

16. Because of his mother's prominent role in his life, songs such as "Brenda's Got a Baby," "Dear Momma," and "Keep Ya Head Up" came from her significant influence in his life.

Hop culture was in its most infant form during this time. Still, Tupac loved Rap music whenever he could listen to it.

The beginning of Tupac's stage presence began at the age of twelve when Afeni enrolled him in a Harlem theater group called The 127th Street Ensemble. This was a key time period in Tupac's life. At age twelve he had his first performance at the famous Apollo Theater. It was at this time Tupac realized that the stage and being in front of people was where he wanted to be.

> When I was young I was quiet, withdrawn. I read a lot, wrote poetry, kept a diary. I watched TV all day. I stayed in front of the television. It was when I was in front of the TV by myself, being alone in the house by myself, having to cook dinner by myself, eat by myself. Just being by myself and looking at TV, at families and all these people out there in this pretend world. I knew I could be part of it if I pretended too, so early on I just watched and emulated . . . and I just thirsted for that. I thought if I could be and act like those characters, act like those people, I could have some of their joy. If I could act like I had a big family I wouldn't feel as lonely.[17]

Tupac had a natural stage presence, and many around him could see that he was different and was going somewhere in life. Still, the issue of poverty was an intensifying one, and Afeni needed to move the family to Baltimore after she lost her job and the family had nowhere to stay.

Baltimore produced more of the same for Tupac: poverty and isolation. Still, in the midst of all of this, Tupac was able to enroll in the School for Performing Arts, and became a top-notch student. More importantly, it was in

17. This was taken from an interview Tupac gave when he was fifteen for a local newspaper.

this school that he was able to develop some of his keen skills on the stage as well as his acting skills.

Rap songs such as LL Cool J's "I'm Bad" and Run DMC's album *Raising Hell* helped to soothe Tupac's harsh reality of life in the inner city. Music was a way out and a way to deal with difficult issues that arose each day living in the ghetto. We begin to see the toll in his early writings as well.

> Life through my bloodshot eyes
> Would scare a square 2 death
> Poverty, murder, violence,
> And never a moment 2 rest
> Fun and games R few
> But treasured like gold 2 me
> Cuz I realize that I must return
> 2 my spot in poverty
> But mock my words when I say
> My heart will not exist
> Unless my destiny comes through
> And puts an end 2 all of this.[18]

We are able to see the passion and zeal that Tupac has for life, all the while that passion is slowly being extinguished by the realities that exist in the ghetto. The arts and music were a way for Tupac to express himself. They helped him through those dark nights, as a therapist would have done with a client.

These are the beginnings of Tupac's musical career. At an early age he was able to develop deep lyrics that shaped his entire life. In each of his songs during this era there is some type of message: an admonition to change, to learn from his mistakes, to gain a broader vision on life, and/or to gain some knowledge on the realities of life around

18. Shakur, *Rose That Grew from Concrete*, 11.

us. This was one of the many reasons why so many young people still love Tupac today and still view him as a cultural icon. Tupac was beginning to place his mark on the culture. The Apollo theater's performance was the first of many that would inspire him to continue with this passion to perform.

The era fades into the next, criminal grind (1981–88) when Tupac and his mother Afeni change locations in the country. Tupac was now aware that the world was not as he thought it was and that Black people were being "dogged" out all over the country and not just on the East Coast.

Criminal Grind (1981–88)

Tupac's criminal grind era does not mean that Tupac was involved with crime, but that his daily life was surrounded with crime. Therefore, that crime element gave him much meaning, identity, perspective, and outlook on the world at large.

Growing Up in Different 'Hoods

In this particular era of Tupac's life, we begin to see the hardness, despair, and gut wrenching realities of the ghetto. Tupac moved from the Bronx to Baltimore after Afeni lost her job and needed a change for the family. Tupac had different feelings about that move, he states:

> . . . and we moved to Baltimore which was total ignorance town to me. It gets me upset to talk about it. . . . Baltimore has the highest rate of teen pregnancy, the highest rate of AIDS within the Black community, the highest rate of teens killing teens, the highest rate of teen suicide, and

> the highest rate of Blacks killing Blacks. And this is where we chose to live.[19]

In this era, Tupac begins to develop his natural skills to Rap. Moreover, in this era, Tupac begins to realize that ghetto poverty is not just in one ghetto, it expands into many.

Here, we can begin to see a strong sense of social justice emerge from Tupac as he sees the differences in each ghetto he is in:

> He's bragging about his new Jordans
> The Baby just ran out of milk
> He's buying gold every 2 weeks
> The baby just ran out of Pampers
> He's buying clothes for his new girl
> and the baby just ran out of medicine
> U ask for money for the Baby
> The Daddy just ran out the Door
> Tears of a Teenage Mother.[20]

Tupac's music has roots in this era. Songs such as "Brenda's Got a Baby,"[21] "Young Black Male," "Crooked Ass Nigga," "Holla If You Hear Me," and "Looking at the World Through My Rearview," to name a few, all connect to this era. All of his albums trace back to these years spending time in different ghettos.

While Tupac was in Baltimore, Afeni enrolled him in The Baltimore School for Performing Arts. He auditioned and made the cut. Tupac's life was now being influenced by

19. This was taken from an interview with Tupac when he was fifteen.

20. Shakur, *Rose That Grew from Concrete*, 101.

21. This particular song deals with the harsh realities of being a single, pregnant, teenage mom. Tupac was heralded for this song, as he presented the "other-side" of sexuality.

other artistic students and by different friends; friends that were not all Black. Tupac was surrounded by Whites, Latinos, and Asians. This helped Tupac to better understand different cultures.

Tupac immersed himself in theater and began to read voraciously. This was a growing period for Tupac's life—he was open for influence and that is what he got. Tupac's influence mainly came from the ghetto streets, but was peppered with artistic values and theater while he was in Baltimore. All of the influence from the streets, hustlers, pimps, and the Panthers were still "in" Tupac's worldview. That element never went away. While some people grow out of their different "eras" Tupac kept a lot of the knowledge and skill gained from each of these eras. This is why he remains one of the most respected Rap artists: authenticity. Still, this was a unique time for Tupac. While in Baltimore, he writes:

> I had a few times when I just zoned out and had good luck. When I auditioned for the Baltimore school for the arts, that was one of my good luck times. I spent three years in Baltimore, my high school years. I loved my classes, made a lot of friends that I wanted to keep over. We were exposed to everything. Theater, ballet, different people's lifestyles—rich people's lifestyles, royalty from other countries and things, everything.[22]

Here Tupac honed his stage presence, polished his natural skill of poetry, and developed a deep sense or knowledge through reading.[23] Tupac began to see that

22. In Shakur et al., *Tupac: Resurrection*.

23. The School for Performing Arts affected Tupac a lot. He loved that school and saw it as a changing point in his life. The school gave him opportunities that many urbanites did or could not have at the time. Tupac excelled in this school. It is interesting to note that Tupac

the world was not equal and fair, nor did the world—America—truly care for the poor and lower class. This strengthened Tupac's sense of social justice, as witnessed throughout his life.

Tupac's sense of awareness was growing at a rapid rate. This fueled him for his career ahead. More importantly, this attitude of life was imparted to others as well. Tupac did not live in the "Hollywood Bubble" that so many do. His home was—as Big Sike and Quincy Jones recall—a refuge and solace for lost souls. Tupac never forgot his "people"—the downtrodden. Rapper and actor Snoop Dogg states, "Tupac was a magnet for lost souls, lost people just knew he would love them—regardless!"[24]

Marin City

After a good friend of Tupac's was shot in Baltimore, Afeni decided to move the family once again to escape that violence. Therefore, in the late 1980s Tupac's family moved to Marin City, California. This was the beginning of a new era in Tupac's life. Tupac hated leaving his beloved school in Maryland. He has been quoted saying, "Leaving that school affected me so much, I see that as the point where I got off track." For Tupac, the ghetto woes did not end on the East Coast, they were just as bad on the West Coast.

> Come to Marin City and there's skinhead violence. There's racial violence, which I deplore. But don't get the wrong idea; I feel like I'm being gloomy. I don't mean to just be like, "Damn it's bad out there." I still try to be positive. I chase girls and want the car and loud music. But I like

never finished high school because he wanted to pursue his career.

24. Taken from *Tupac: Resurrection*, DVD, audio (2003).

> to think of myself as socially aware. I think there should be a drug class, a sex education class. A real sex education class. A class on police brutality. There should be a class on why people are hungry, but there are not. There are classes on . . . gym. Physical education. Let's learn volleyball.[25]

The streets of Marin City influence Tupac extensively. In a 1992 interview with Davey D, Tupac states:

> Being in Marin City was like a small town so it taught me to be more straightforward with my style. Instead of being so metaphorical with the rhyme, where I might say something like, "I'm the hysterical, lyrical miracle. I'm the hypothetical, incredible," I was encouraged to go straight at it and hit it dead on and not waste time trying to cover things.[26]

Tupac enrolled in public school and he began to realize that they had left nothing in Baltimore, the same element that Tupac despised was present here in Marin City: poverty. To compound the situation, the political economy of crack cocaine was in full swing. More importantly, Afeni the activist was now becoming Afeni the addict. Afeni, Tupac's "homie" and mom, was now addicted to crack cocaine. And as some have stated, "was now breaking into the republican political régime with crack."[27]

25. This was part of an interview when Tupac was fifteen.

26. Taken from the 1992 "lost interview with Tupac Shakur" by Davey D—renowned Hip Hop DJ and B-Boy.

27. Tupac's brother, in Peters, *Tupac Vs.*

The Political Economy of Crack Cocaine

Crack cocaine became a commodity that many in the ghetto fought for and died for. Both Black and Brown people were vying for this new commodity that manifested itself in a small "tic-tac" like substance called crack. Tupac was firsthand witness to this. Michael Dyson states:

> Then what you get in the '80s is the political economy of crack. Crack crimes, addictions, and people began to organize their lives in these terror enclaves called ghettos.
>
> The reality of it was that the community was drenched with crack. The government turned a deaf ear and eye to what was happening in the ghettos across America. The crack economy created hostility between Black and Brown families. . . . Joseph Marshall states that crack cocaine did what 300 years of slavery could not do. It undermined and subverted the integrity of the black family by virtue of creating a commodity over which black people were literally killing themselves to get access to. And Pac had to watch that contradiction within his own mother of the Black revolution. On the one hand you had the promise to make it and succeed, and on the other hand the capitulation to the worst form of anti-revolutionary there was, that is addiction.[28]

Moreover, Tupac had to witness his "homie" or best friend—his mother Afeni—became broke down by this addiction. "My mom, she was lost at that particular moment. She wasn't caring for herself. She was addicted to crack. It was a hard time, because she was my hero." For Tupac, to see such a revolutionary person like his mother—who

28. Dyson in Peters, *Tupac Vs.*

once stood for independence and freedom—now stricken with an addiction, was hardening his soul.

This was a difficult time for Tupac. Many of his friends during this era state that this was the point in which Tupac began to feel depressed and became real hurt and dismayed about life.[29] He was discouraged and began to feel as though the world was just too hard to live in. There were thoughts of suicide and there was much pain in his life at this time.[30]

The travesty of Afeni's addiction was also coupled with the fact that he had to go to a "ghetto" high school. He longed to go back to the performing arts school, but now he was faced with what so many urban youth are faced with still today: underrepresented and under-sourced schools. During this era, Tupac began to develop a cornerstone in his mantra; it was the mantra of "fuck it" and "fuck the world." Years of pain, misery, hurt, and despair led him to finally begin to feel as though America did not care. In my estimation there was a fundamental shift in Tupac's attitude in late 1987. The once bright-eyed and hopeful idealist was now saying "fuck you" to the whole world—and the ghetto was backing him.

This was a shift in Tupac's worldview once again: from idealistic and hopeful, to a negative and vengeful outlook. Afeni's crack addiction was taking its toll on Tupac. Crack cocaine and its vicious distress on the Black and urban

29. E.g., Peters, *Tupac Vs.*, and personal interviews with friends who stayed with Tupac's family during this era.

30. The 1980s crime and crack wave was an unrivaled phenomenon. Crime and murders today are nothing compared to the crime and violence that existed in urban communities during this decade. As I grew up in this decade, I saw firsthand what crack can do to a family member, and how violent the streets really are. That element was even more powerful in cites such as Marin City and East Oakland where Tupac was raised and spent a majority of his years.

communities were too much for him. In certain poems he wrote, "The only way 2 change me is maybe blow my brains out. Stuck in the middle of the game, come and get the pain out."[31]

Ghetto Mindset

Around late 1987 and early 1988, we begin to see Tupac's life changing. He is fighting a lot more, there is more weed smoking, and there is a lot more frivolous living. Marin City was taking its toll on Tupac. For many, especially those with even less hope and vision than Tupac, they cannot escape this enclave of horror. They simply end up a statistic. However, for Tupac, music was his savior and music helped him through those rough times.

In Tupac's writings and poems during this time, there is a shift from being positive to more gloomy. Tupac was on his own and being taken care of by people who he was used to: the thugs, gang members, pimps, and hustlers of the 'hood. Tupac states:

> All my songs deal with pain. That's what makes me, that's what makes me do what I do. Everything is based on the pain I felt in my childhood. Small pieces of it and harsh pieces of it. My inspiration for writing music is like Don Mclean did when he did "American Pie" or "Vincent." Lorraine Hansberry with *A Raisin in the Sun*. Like Shakespeare when he does his thing, like deep stories, like raw human needs.[32]

Part of the Ghetto mindset is rooted in Black nationalism, where on one side of the table is the ideology of "how

31. Shakur, *Rose That Grew from Concrete*, 71.

32. Shakur et al., *Tupac: Resurrection*, 70.

to get paid" using American capitalism, while on the other side is the struggle of identifying and helping fellow Black people. Tupac was now consumed with trying to rise above his current situation and gain knowledge at any cost. He was inspired to get out of the lifestyle he and his family was living. The only means he saw to do that was music. While others around him were just giving in to the pressure of ghetto life, Tupac used his experiences to inspire him to write magnificent songs that would later become hits for the Hip Hop community and would change the Hip Hop cultural continuum forever. He now begins to take on one of the three roles in his music (as seen in Table 2).[33]

Table 2: Tupac's Musical Positions

Observer	When Pac is involved in the story he is telling, he is typically telling it in first person: involved in what is going on. The song "How Long Will They Mourn Me?" is an example.
Participant	Pac is telling the story from a second or even third person point of view. He is merely observing what is going on in the culture or in a particular context. Songs like "Dear Momma" are a good example of Pac observing reality as he sees it.
Messenger	Here Pac is telling a message about what is going to happen, what has happened, or what is happening. This is where Pac is considered to be a prophet. Songs like "If I Die Tonight" (which actually predicted his death over some real dumb stuff) is an example.

Here we are able to gain more insight into how Tupac's music is broken down. For Tupac, there was never a time to make a song that did not have some type of meaning in it. Even songs like "I Get Around" and "How Do You

33. Taken directly from Hodge, "Insights from Tupac."

Want It" had a message inside of them. They went beyond the typical gangsta, party Rap style that so many rappers are stuck in today.

Tupac's musical influence originated from several key elements seen in Figure 2. First, he was the child of a passionate revolutionary. Second, he was raised poor. That in itself is an entire book or album. Growing up poor makes the individual either rise to magnificent heights, or breaks the person down so much that the only hope they have is a government check and twenty dollar ride. Third, Afeni had been on crack. Crack cocaine demoralizes a person. And while all of us are held accountable for our decisions, Afeni's situation might have been different had she had different opportunities and outlets in her life. More importantly, one must ask the question, "What if she had been living in a better neighborhood, stronger community, and had a different socioeconomic background? Would she have not been an addict?" Fourth, Tupac had a father who was steeped in the thug traditions of the ghetto. The values, cares, and concerns of the street were etched into Tupac's mind, social construct, and soul. These would never leave him. As he put it, "The thugs shown me love, so until you all [speaking to a crowd of Black adults] begin to step up and help raise us, I don't want to hear fuck about it." All four of these areas shaped Tupac's life in this era and are the cornerstone of his musical and acting career until his death in 1996.

At the end of this era Tupac is rising to popularity with the Rap group Digital Underground. Tupac is now touring and rapping with this group and gaining some fame. This era ends when Tupac begins to see the media as a source for helping the 'hood through Rap videos. This was a shift that led to his next era: the ghetto is destiny (1989–1992).

Figure 2: Tupac's Musical Foundation

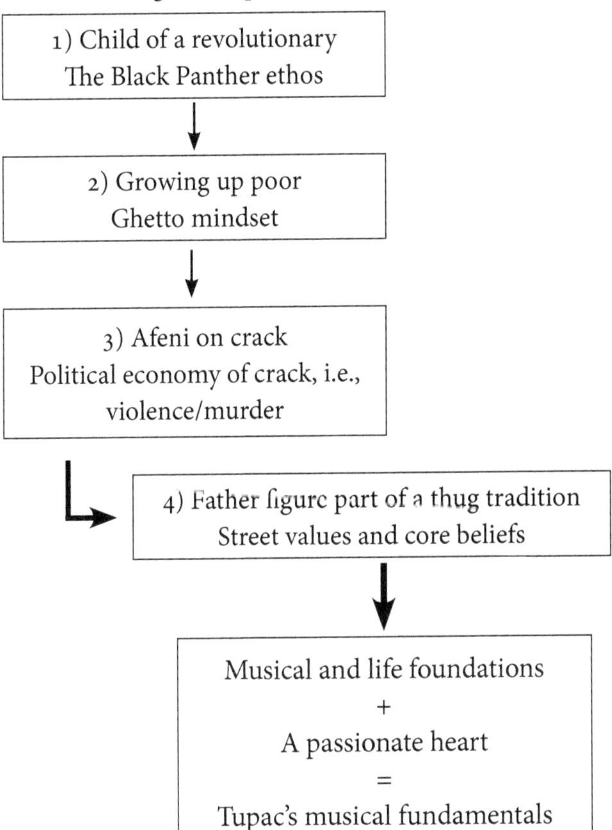

The Ghetto Is Destiny (1989–92)

This era saw Tupac glamorizing the ghetto within his music. Tupac felt as though the advent of music videos was a poster board of sorts, to help effect change in the ghetto.

For Tupac, the ghetto was his destiny, and he wanted to tell the world about it.

The Era: Sources of Tupac's Passion and Vision

Tupac makes an amazing statement about this era in his life:

> It's like, you've got the Vietnam War, and because you had reporters showing us pictures of the war at home, that's what made the war end, or that shit would have lasted longer. If no one knew what was going on we would have thought they were just dying valiantly in some beautiful way. But because we saw the horror, that's what made us stop the war. So I thought, that's what I'm going to do as an artist, as a rapper I'm gonna show the most graphic details of what I see in my community and hopefully they'll stop it quick. I've seen all of that—the crack babies, what we had to go through, losing everything, being poor, and getting beat down. All of that. Being the person I am, I said no no no no. I'm changing this![34]

This era in Tupac's life begins with him being introduced to a community leader named Leila Stenberg. Leila—another woman—was a significant influence in Tupac's life. She was married, had kids, and was living a steady life in Marin County. Tupac, while he was homeless and living from house to house, came to live with Leila and her family for quite some time. Leila first spotted Tupac rapping at a community show, and from then on she had him come to her poetry night for young people.

34. Tabitha Soren interview from 1994, in Lazin, *Tupac: Resurrection.*

Tupac was on fire at this point. He used all of his past experiences to infuse his lyrics with a combination of social justice, comedy, and theology. Tupac was on the road to a great Rap career. He continued to grow in his lyrical skills as well.

Dyson states that the ghetto was the source and major metaphor of Tupac's music and life. For Tupac, the ghetto was a wide-open storybook that needed to be told. Tupac felt that the story needed to be ushered into the living rooms of White America. It is from this notion that White Americans began to get their first taste of what Black life was all about. This is the reason why so many suburban Whites idolize Tupac just as much as urban youth do. Quincy Jones said that you cannot sell forty million records without someone who is White buying them. White youth today know Tupac well because of the reality that he spoke, the authenticity he brings, and the universal sentiment of being caged—whether in the terrenes of the ghetto or behind the pristine gates of suburbia—White youth know an authentic person when they see one.

Let's look at this in another sense. Ester Iverem writes:

> Affinity for Tupac mixes what is potentially a positive attitude toward self determination with the worst definitions of that over used phrase: Keep it Real. At its most meaningful, the phrase urges those in the hip hop nation to remain true to their beliefs and rooted in reality. At its worst, it implies that only those things ghetto-centric and hard are real in black culture. It endorses the use of street ethics to settle disputes, like the willingness to bust a cap in someone, usually another African-American, if necessary.[35]

35. Iverem, "Politics of 'Fuck It,'" 42.

Tupac embodied the struggle between the positive Black awareness and Black pride on the one hand, while on the other he had the thug, ghetto mindset and "fuck-you" attitude that manifests itself in so many young, Black males. Tupac's ghetto-centric values drove him to great success with the Hip Hop generation.

Tupac's worldview came through in early works such as "Panther Power":

> As real as it seems the American Dream
> Ain't nothing but another calculated schemes
> To get us locked up shot up back in chains
> To deny us of the future rob our names
> Kept my history of mystery but now I see
> The American Dream wasn't meant for me
> Cause lady liberty is a hypocrite she lied to me
> Promised me freedom, education, equality
> Never gave me nothing but slavery
> And now look at how dangerous you made me
> Calling me a mad man cause I'm strong and bold.

In this particular piece, performed at a Black Panther rally in East Oakland, Tupac's passion and knowledge begins to take shape in his music. All of the pent up anger and pain was beginning to come through in his music. As much as many older Blacks do not want to admit it—especially those born prior to 1970—Tupac reflected Black theology. A theology that says that Black people have a place, too, at the throne of God. More importantly we must assert that position and fight to keep it. Tupac knew the Bible inside out; he had grown up with it and was raised in the ways of the Lord. He was simply vocalizing a cry, which had gone unheard for too long. Dyson writes, "Tupac was obsessed with God. His lyrics drip with a sense of the divine. . . . Tupac's spiritual matters never left him, although its form and function in his later life may have become almost unrecognizable by earlier standards."[36]

Death

There is an admiration in the 'hood with regards to death. It is valued, feared at times, and also glamorized. Dyson says:

> The sheer repetition of death has caused black youth to execute funeral plans. In its response to death, black youth have reversed perhaps the emblematic expression of self-aware black morality. Martin Luther King Jr.'s cry that "every now and then I think about my own death." They think about it constantly and creatively. With astonishing clinical detachment, black youth enliven King's claim that he didn't contemplate his death "in a morbid sense." They accept the bleak inevitability of death's imminent swoop—which, in truth, is a rejection of the arbitrariness we all face, since death to these youth is viewed as the condition, not the culmination, of their existence. Black youth tell funeral directors to portray their dead bodies with a style that may defeat their being forgotten and that distinguish them from the next corpse.[37]

For Tupac, death was a constant. In his song "Death on Every Corner," Tupac depicts death that is an ongoing event.

> I see death around the corner, gotta stay high while I
> survive
> In the city where the skinny niggas die

36. Dyson, *Holler If You Hear Me*, 201.

37. Peters, *Tupac Vs.*

If they bury me, bury me as a G nigga, no need to
worry
I expect retaliation in a hurry
I see death around the—corner, any day
Tryin to keep it together, no one lives forever anyway
Strugglin and strivin, my destiny's to die
Keep my finger on the trigger, no mercy in my eyes.

Tupac continued to Rap about the horrors and pleasures of death. On one track you might have him rapping about the horrible death of a friend, while on the other he is rapping about the joy of finally being free.

For many ethnic-minority youth, death is a time to rest. Death is a time to finally be out of the hell called the ghetto. Regardless, Tupac wanted to help provide some context and language for that. But, as one can imagine, he didn't know the precise language or means to do that; especially when a lot of his friends were dying. Tupac states, "Don't feel bad for the people that died, Feel bad for the folk that gotta stay behind. They the ones still in hell. The person who's dead is now at peace, and in joy, finally resting."

Digital Underground

Around the late 1980s, Tupac was introduced to the famed Rap group Digital Underground. This was the start of Tupac's professional career as a Rap artist. He started very humbly. It was a time where he developed a rigorous work ethic. Many in Hip Hop culture referred to Tupac as the hardest working man in Hip Hop. He was not married, had no kids, and did not have the typical responsibilities of that came with these attachments. In this way there is some parallel between Tupac and the Apostle Paul.

Leila introduced Tupac to the manager of Digital Underground. Tupac states:

> This lady named Leila introduced me to Atron Gregory who was managing Digital Underground. He was like, "Ima send you to Digital Underground, they in the studio. You just rap for Shock G on the spot. If he likes you, Ima pick you up." I just walked in and rapped for him. He's like, "Ok, good, you're in, boom-boom-boom, I'll see you later." I just walked out of there like, dang! I look back with the greatest fondness. Those were like some of the best times in my life. It's all funny to me, it's all good. The silly part is like me running around in zebra print underwears, and making simulated sex. We had like the funniest, craziest show. Think hip-hop needs another Digital Underground right now. As soon as I got a chance to say what was on my mind, I said what was on my mind and we have a platinum record now. So I went from dancing naked with dolls, being unknown, to having a platinum record.[38]

Tupac was on the road to success. Digital Underground paved the way. Tupac was able to meet a lot of important people in the industry and began to be well known. For Tupac, this was another opportunity to help his people and his family. Tupac began to send checks home to his family. He paid their bills, their rent, helped his mom get off crack, and bought homes for them. While many rappers would have taken the money and spent it on frivolous things, Tupac saved and spent it on "the people." Tupac helped many in need with his newfound fame, strengthening his authenticity within the urban and Hip

38. From a 1993 interview, interviewer unknown.

Hop communities. Shock G, of Digital Underground, said, "Tupac didn't care about the mundane things in life like new rugs, gold, and new things in general. He was like, man check this new beat out, or shit, this new rhyme is dope right? Tupac was on another level; something we can't even comprehend."

Tupac got a track on the song "Same Song." After which, he dropped his first solo album *2Pacalypse Now*. This album laid out much of his early childhood struggles, and Digital Underground helped produce most of the album

2Pacalypse Now

In a 1992 interview with Davey D, Tupac talks about this new album. Tupac stated that this album was for the nigga, the real niggas, and that he wanted to give insight into the life of a Black man. Tupac dedicated this album to the working class Black person. Tupac remained who he was. In fact it brought him no better pleasure than to have people see him at a club or house party the same night he was in concert. Tupac and The Black Panther Party's mantra of "being for the people" was manifesting itself in the way Tupac lived his life.

Further, with this new album, young people in the Hip Hop community began to see Tupac as the ghetto prophet. *2Pacalypse Now* sparked many conversations such as these. With songs such as "Young Black Male," "Brenda's Got a Baby," and "Trapped" Tupac began to be seen as the irreverent theologian. This irreverence, or the profane, is no mystery to Blacks. In fact, most early Black gospel music was considered profane and indecent in comparison to White gospel music. For many Blacks, they had to have church without any set "ordained" pastor, because some denominations would not ordain a Black minister. Tupac faced the same dilemma, except this time it was not a White audience condemning Tupac's music, it was a Black audience.

T.H.U.G. L.I.F.E.

It is around this time that Tupac, after seeing violence erupt in his home town (Marin City) and different concerts, developed the code for THUG LIFE. THUG LIFE for Tupac stood for "The Hate U Give Little Infants Fucks Everyone." It was a code for the streets. It was a way to organize the different 'hoods and get those involved in the underground economy on one accord. Tupac knew that no one else had a heart for the ghetto, so he decided to take matters into his own hands and deal with the problems straight on. He states:

> There was no spot for Tupac. Its not like there was somebody like me before and I moved into the spot so I can ask him how he did it. There was no spot here. Nobody wanted to be the person the thugs and the street people could rally around nobody wanted to be that. So when I was that, I couldn't handle it. I could handle it, but not right away.
>
> I'm twenty two. I was havin' concerts, they was sold out—white boys, Mexicans, Blacks and they would all do whatever I said. I could tell all those people in the audience "Turn around in a circle" and they would do it. I was havin' love, undeniable love, and I was scared. I was so scared that I would come to a town and I would have the leader of the gang there tellin me, "What you need?"

> But that makes me rise to the occasion.
> Makes me wanna give my whole life to 'em, and
> I will give my whole life to this plan I have for
> Thug Life.[39]

For Tupac, the thug did not mean the criminal, the fool, the person who is robbing old ladies or stealing cars. For Tupac, it meant the underdog. The person who has never had anything. People who knew Tupac intimately agreed with this assessment. Many state that their own family members called them "little hoodlums" and "thugs" so, in turn, they lived up to the label. Tupac wanted to end crime and violence. However, he soon realized that it was not going to just end. Tupac then figured that it could at least be organized; gangs, pimps, hustlers, or people in the "game" could at least give back to the neighborhood they were raping. Tupac decided there needed to be a street code for the 'hood.

Tupac argued that if the person who has nothing succeeds, then he was a thug because he overcame all the obstacles in life. For Tupac, the word "thug" had nothing to do with the dictionary's definition of "thug." Tupac states, "I know it's not good, violence ain't good. It's just there are certain situations that there is no way out. There is a way out, but until we can find that way out, then there is no way to stop talking about this type of lifestyle."

Tupac, once again, made the ghetto a stage in this era. He set up the ghetto in a way that other Hip Hop artists had not done in the past. N.W.A. had spoke on police brutality, Ice Cube spoke on the injustices experienced by young Black males, and Ice T constantly warned the United States about the anger and despair boiling over in the ghettos. Tupac took that a step further and made the ghetto into a

39 From 1995 interview in prison; see Peters, *Tupac Vs.*

show. Tupac was able to reach deeper into Middle America and let those people know that there were separate societies that existed in the United States.

Tupac states about THUG LIFE and ghetto life:

> You know what gang violence is, I'm gonna tell you, and people don't want you to hear this; someone shoots your family member, then of course you retaliate. Same thing US does, except no one shot they family members. They shoot up some school or something, then the US says we gotta go help them and show them who the real killas are, that's the same mentality these gangsters have. The US is the biggest gang in the world, look what they did to Cuba, they didn't agree with Cuba so they blocked them off. That's what we do on the street.[40]

THUG LIFE set a precedent that would stick with Tupac the rest of his career. His heart beat for THUG LIFE. Tupac felt as though America did not have any room to criticize him about this mantra of his. "What makes me saying 'I don't give a fuck' different from Patrick Henry saying 'give me liberty or give me death?' What makes my freedom less worth fighting for than Bosnians?"

THUG LIFE did not want to "clean-up" any young Black male. THUG LIFE took them as they were: raw, stinking, foul, and open to change (a Christ-like value from where I stand); yet another reason that Tupac is considered a ghetto saint. This Christ-like value is still heard in today's Hip Hop culture and Rap music and artists like Kendrick Lamar carry the mantle Tupac started.

40. Tabitha Soren interview from 1994 in Lazin, *Tupac: Resurrection.*

Exodus 18:11

Finally, we have the scripture of Exodus 18:11 tattooed on the back of Tupac's back. This scripture was a staple for Tupac's mantra. He felt as though God would have his wrath on those who misused their power and authority, and urbanites would have justice. Tupac constantly referred to Old Testament images of God; a God that would take revenge and kill his enemies. Dyson writes:

> The gangsta's God—or the thug's theology—is internally linked to his beliefs about how society operates and who is in control. For many thugs, God is the great accomplice to a violent lifestyle. . . . This may ring true for the vengeful deity depicted in the Old Testament, where the principle of a life for a life prevailed. But the last couple of millennia have witnessed a transformation of God's image. To an extent, thug theology is willfully anachronistic or at least staunchly traditional.[41]

THUG LIFE was intrinsically connected back to God and Exodus 18:11. God would take revenge. "He did this to those who treated Israel arrogantly" (NIV) was how Tupac viewed the "promise-land" for young Black youth.

Exodus 18:11 provided hope. And Tupac, as much as he loved the ghetto, searched for a way out of this style of living. He himself said that no one really wants to live there, no one really is talking about "killing each other for fun." This gave many young people hope and vision for a gloomy tomorrow; Tupac was part of that hope and Tupac would continually point to God.

Exodus 18:11 developed around the early 1990s, when political and conscious Rap were beginning to take

41. Dyson, *Holler If You Hear Me*, 234.

shape in Hip Hop culture. This was a significant event in the making. Several years later Tupac recorded and rapped the song "I Wonder if Heaven Got a Ghetto?" In this track Tupac made several references to peace, rest, retribution, and a place for everyone to "chill" and take it easy. The Exodus 18:11 theme stayed with Tupac and the people around him. After seeing the firsthand hardships his family and friends faced living in the ghetto, Tupac had to have something to hold on to, this was Exodus 18:11.

It is during the latter part of 1991 that Tupac's life begins to change once again. Tupac had his first major encounter with the law in 1992 with the Oakland Police Department. Tupac, up until this point, had never experienced police brutality firsthand, nor many of the negative interactions with the law he had rapped about in many of his songs. Tupac's life would be changed forever, and it was now that he was moving into his next life stage, outlaw.

Outlaw (1992–95)

This era finds Tupac in trouble with the law. It seemed between these years that Tupac was in and out of trouble with the criminal justice system. For many years, Tupac had only rapped about being an outlaw, but Tupac's vision became reality between these years.

The Long Arm of the Law

The talent that Tupac developed in his early years at the school for performing arts in Baltimore was beginning to flourish in American popular culture. Hip Hop culture as a whole was experiencing an influx of suburban Whites that were falling in love with Rap music. The early to mid

1990s gave White America a glimpse into Black America, and it was exotic. Hip Hop culture was also growing and flowing into suburban homes. As Quincy Jones once said, "You can't sell over ten million records without somebody White buying them!" Tupac's "thug" persona was fitting into American popular culture. Moreover, that persona was gaining momentum in an era in American popular culture that saw the rise of Hip Hop culture and Rap music. The "Black-Bad-Boy" image was on the rise in America, and Tupac was leading the way.

Tupac's interaction with the law and criminal justice system only strengthened his street credibility and Hip Hop authenticity. For Tupac, during this era, he felt as though he was the leader of a THUG LIFE nation: a nation that was going to rebuild the ghettos and restructure the United States Black communities. For Tupac, this era was a significant milestone to gain his street credibility and to further the THUG LIFE cause.

In this particular era of Tupac's life, we begin to see a pattern of "outlawish" activities—while not insinuating that he was a criminal—Tupac had some areas that were causing him problems in his life. During these years, Tupac's life was adversely affected. He felt that he was the spokesperson for Blacks and the ghetto community. During this time, however, he began to receive much criticism from the Black community about his lyrics, lifestyle, thug persona, and his seemingly violent behavior; this was mainly from older Blacks, ages thirty and up—mainly from the civil rights generation.

Tupac's THUG LIFE credibility was boosted when he went to jail. Moreover, his vigor and fighting personality made him a spokesperson for THUG LIFE and for resisting the law as a whole. His fight against corrupt police was also strengthened during this era. Tupac constantly encouraged young Black males, to take up "arms" against corrupt police. Tupac's legal troubles were also a result of his "big mouth" that he so often admitted he had.[42] We see this trend of incidents (that more than likely could have been avoided) emerge from Tupac's life during this particular era of Tupac's life.

It is during this era that the deep rage, anger, and despair that engulfed his life emerged through these incidents. Tupac's life was nothing more than a mirror of the rage, despair, and anger that so many young Black males have and still feel to this day.

Hollywood

Tupac made his film debut in *Juice* (1992). In this particular film, Tupac played the troubled teen named Bishop. Bishop's life was consumed with making a name for himself and attaining the "juice"—that is, the respect and admiration that so many young people in the ghetto need. Bishop eventually went crazy with power, and he killed his best friend and injured another before falling to his death at the end of the film. Tupac fit this role eerily well. His persona made the character so believable that Tupac's image was now marked for life; people began to believe that Tupac was that crazy, cold-hearted, and manipulative person that "Bishop" was. This could not have been further from the truth. But, as Appendix H illustrates in Tupac's involvement with the criminal justice system, if one was to follow simply the "facts" and the "stats" then they could only assume that "if the shoe fits. . ." Moreover, the fact that Tupac was Black only added to this characterization.

42. Shakur et al., *Tupac Resurrection*, 120.

The media did not have any less pity on Tupac's image. They merely reinforced the stereotype that Tupac was a street hoodlum and "thug." Still, Hollywood was a perfect fit for Tupac, and it was during this era that Tupac's silver screen performances began to grow. Even though Tupac never graduated, the years spent at the Baltimore School for Performing Arts were paying off. Tupac states about Bishop's character:

> Bishop is a psychopath, but, more true to his character, Bishop is a lonely, misguided young kid. His heroes are James Cagney and Scarface, those kinds of guys. Shoot'-em-up, go-out-in-a-blaze type of gangsters. I don't think acting is as technical as they try to make it. They try and make it technical so everybody isn't an actor. All you really have to do is feel for your character and relate to your character. Because when you act you satisfy inside of yourself. The character is me, I'm Bishop. Everybody got a little Bishop in them.[43]

Tupac wanted to give the public a glimpse into the harsh realities of ghetto life for young Black males. He wanted to let others know of the hardships, and Hollywood was just another open outlet for that expression. The early 1990s were filled with revolt, anger, political upheaval, and a nation that had to deal with the harsh realities of racism and a growing anger from the 'hood. These forces, coupled with the United States's refusal to acknowledge a ghetto problem, helped to shape part of Tupac's worldview during this era of his life. It is also interesting to note that the image of Bishop in *Juice*, would follow Tupac to his grave. Many assumed Tupac to be that same character in real life.

43. YO MTV Raps interview, 1994, in Lazin, *Tupac: Resurrection*.

Tupac took another sharp turn in characters in the film *Poetic Justice* (1993), which put him opposite Janet Jackson. His character, Lucky, was in stark contrast to Bishop. Lucky was responsible, talented, caring, and goal-oriented. Tupac states:

> If Bishop was a reflection of young Black male today, I wouldn't be honest if I didn't show another reflection. All of our young Black males are not violent, they're all not taking the law into their own hands. Lucky is doing it the opposite way that Bishop did. He's working, he's very responsible. He's very deliberate about the things he's doing. He's taking care of his daughter. He's a respectful person, you know what I'm saying? He lives at home with his mother, he's not sweating it, that's where he wants to be. He wants to work.[44]

Hollywood gave Tupac more creative freedom. It also made him a stronger pop culture figure. Many young Whites were seeing Tupac on the silver screen for the first time and they loved him. During this era, there was also a shift in American pop culture from what was considered "White" to Black popular culture. Tupac entered the homes of many young White Gen Xers. This not only increased his record sales, but also gave him a voice to a different audience that was not primarily Black or Latino. White youth were seeing different sides of Tupac.

Tupac embodied the rebel, idealist, socialist, and social activist that so many White Gen X youth were craving. More importantly, White Gen X youth could relate to some of his pain in the sense that they too had been rejected, broken, and discarded by society. Poor White youth

44. YO MTV Raps interview, 1994, in Lazin, *Tupac: Resurrection*.

could especially relate to Tupac because they faced some of the same economic depravities that Blacks and Latinos faced. Tupac was a hero for them as well. Hollywood gave Tupac an opportunity to express his voice and message to White Gen X youth.

Tupac completed work on six films: *Juice* (1992), *Poetic Justice* (1993), *Above the Rim* (1994), *Bullet* (1996), *Gridlock'd* (1997), and *Gang Related* (1997). All these films helped Tupac connect with a larger audience in America. These films are still classics for many urban audiences, not because of the excellent screenplays or directing—while some of the films were good in those areas—but because Tupac was in the film. He brought realism to the cinema that was unrivaled. Tupac had dreams to write several different screenplays and was in the process of putting together several films that he was going to direct when his sudden death came in 1996. Tupac talks about his fame:

> Being famous and having money gave me confidence. The screams of the crowd gave me confidence. Before that I was a shell of a man. Now I believe that I'm my own man. I put it down, I put it down. If it's about rap music, if its about acting whatever—I want to get into the head set, I gotta be involved, I gotta excel at it.[45]

THUG LIFE and Hollywood

THUG LIFE only grew while Tupac was doing film and gaining notoriety. THUG LIFE was at its height while America, during the late '80s and early '90s, was coming to grips with how to deal with the image of the young Black male that said "I don't give a fuck!" Hollywood, during this

45. YO MTV Raps Interview, 1994, in Lazin, *Tupac: Resurrection.*

period, was releasing numerous gangsta films. Films such as *Boyz in the Hood* (1991), *Menace II Society* (1993), and *Belly* (1994) were just a few of the ones that made headlines. These hard-core snapshots of firsthand ghetto horror gave Tupac and his THUG LIFE code a platform on which to speak. The years between 1992 and '94 were tumultuous times for American culture. These years were filled with political stands from the inner-city community and from activist voices such as Ice Cube and KRS-One.

THUG LIFE was hot, and Hollywood, White Gen X youth, and Rap music fueled the flames. Still, this did not come without criticism. Tupac faced many critics that claimed he was only inciting hoodlum behavior. Even civil rights leaders such as Jesse Jackson criticized Tupac for the power and use of his lyrics in such songs as "Fuck the World" and "Outlaw." Delores Tucker publicly advocated that Tupac should be banned and that it was a disgrace when he won an NAACP image award. Regardless, through all of this, Tupac persisted.

For Tupac, THUG LIFE was more than just an "era" or movement. For him, and the millions that loved him, it was a way of life. In a moving statement, Tupac says this about THUG LIFE and his image:

> I don't rap about sitting up eating shrimp and shit. I rap about fighting back. I make it uncomfortable by putting details to it. It might not have been politically correct but I've reached somebody; they relating to me. They relate to the brutal honesty in the rap. And why shouldn't they be angry? And why shouldn't my raps that I'm rappin' to my community be filled with rage? They should be filled with the same atrocities that they gave me. You have to be logical. If I know that in this hotel room, they have food

> everyday and I'm knockin' on the door everyday to eat and they open the door and let me see the party—see like them throwin' salami all over, just like throwin' food around—then they're tellin' me there's no food in there, you know what I'm sayin'? Everyday. I'm standing outside trying to sing my way in. "We are hungry please let us in, we are hungry, please let us in." After about a week that song is going to change to "We hungry, we need some food." After two, three weeks it's like "Give me some food, we're bangin' on the door." After a year its like, "I'm pickin' the lock, comin' through the door blastin," you know what I'm sayin'? It's like you hungry you've reached your level. You don't want anymore. We asked ten years ago. We was askin' with the Panthers. We was askin' them with the civil rights movement. We was askin', you know? Now those people who was askin' are all dead or in jail. Now what do you think we're going to do? Ask? . . . I have not brought violence to you or thug life to America. Why am I being persecuted?[46]

Tupac had decided long ago to fight his war using the weapons of media. He saw the power to reach the masses behind the camera and on the microphone. He understood the power of mass media, and used it to its full potential.

Prison and Me Against the World

For Tupac, being in prison was a life-changing event. His music, life, poetry, and countenance are adversely affected as a result of this. It is during this era and and as a result of this event that Tupac takes the popular stance that

46. Interview with Tabitha Soren, 1994, in Lazin, *Tupac: Resurrection.*

most who have not studied him know: namely "fuck the world." In late 1994, Tupac released his album *Me Against the World*. Tupac's life was changing and these life trials were taking a toll on him. People like Bob Dole, C. Delores Tucker, and Dan Quayle were beginning to wear on Tupac. He states, "They don't even know what they talkin'. They just talking. They could be talking about Bob Marley for all they care. . . . I know somebody geesed them up to attack Tupac, and now what it does is, they attacked a few famous rappers and now they themselves are famous."

Prison took its toll on Tupac. For those around him, they admit it was a turning point in his life. He was sent to prison in 1994 to serve a jail term for "forcibly touching the buttocks." During this time Tupac once again began to see the world differently. He felt as though he did not have friends anymore. He states:

> I don't have any friends anymore. I'm surrounded, but I don't have any friends. I have homies, associates. What relationship could I possibly have? Now I'm petrified; I can't mess with women. Now, I'm vulnerable cuz they all like, "Ah ha! You're in trouble." So I just decided to withdraw myself.[47]

Tupac's life was severely affected by prison and his life was changed. There were rumors that he was raped in prison. Rumors that he denies, but nonetheless exist; these hurt Tupac deeply. He further states:

> Prison kills your sprit, there is no creativity. . . . I see a lot of it in other prisoners . . . but as for me, I am not there. I am reflecting back on life, prison doesn't inspire creativity.

47. From Clinton Correctional Facility Prison Interview, September 1995: https://www.youtube.com/watch?v=nhpq0MEcYzg.

> Do not come to jail, this is not the spot, I am surrounded with dudes that made a mistake when they were young and now in here for life. Do whatever you have to do to stay the hell out of here. I am a messenger, you know, if I go to a club I tell you the club is poppin' or the club is sorry. . . . This ain't the spot, its like you an animal, no man don't wanna be here or a woman.[48]

For Tupac, this was a time to reflect on his life. He engrossed himself in reading and listening to music. Upon his release, he dropped the album *Me Against the World* and songs like "Me Against the World" made headlines. Tupac wrote only one song while in prison, he said that he could not write at the time. However, within a matter of two weeks after his release, he had written twenty-four songs. Below is the first lyrics from "Me Against the World":

> Can you picture my prophecy?
> Stress in the city, the cops is hot for me
> The projects is full of bullets, the bodies is droppin
> There ain't no stoppin me
> Constantly movin while makin millions
> Witnessin killings, leavin dead bodies in abandoned buildings
> Carries to children cause they're illin
> Addicted to killin and the appeal from the cap peelin.

This album provided a release for Tupac. It was a release of his raw emotions that had been kept inside while in prison. This album was a way for his artistic side to come out and to exonerate his character. Tupac did not want to die before people knew that he did not commit the crimes he had been sent to prison for. Tupac always maintained his innocence throughout all of this.

48. From Clinton Correctional Facility Prison Interview, September 1995: https://www.youtube.com/watch?v=nhpq0MEcYzg.

Tupac was bailed out of prison by Suge Knight, the president of Death Row Records. It was late 1995 when Tupac entered into his final era of life, ghetto saint. As Tupac drew closer to his death, his studio hours increased and between his release from prison and the time of his death on September 13, 1996, he recorded over 120 songs. His sainthood was forming as he entered into his life's final stage.

Ghetto Saint (1996–Present)

Much of Tupac's work has been published and released posthumously. However, he wrote and produced that work during this era. This era finds Tupac's legendary status taking shape and deals with how Tupac's ghetto saint status took shape. This era could be broken into several others as well, but for the sake of this book, I will keep it to one.

All Eyez on Him

As a contextual saint that helped push his listeners closer to God, Tupac realized the extent of racism and White oppression and wanted to do something more about it beyond just music and movies. This created a sense of urgency for him that was unmatched in any of his peers at the time. Some might say this was the era Tupac produced his greatest work. Tupac's ghetto saint status began to form in the last year of his life: 1996. Tupac's decision to sign with Death Row Records, after his release from prison, brought with it many problems and difficulties. During the beginning of this era, Tupac faced many moral and ethical decisions. Yet because his face was in the public eye, more people got to know and love him because of his struggles.

Tupac makes a poignant statement regarding his lifestyle during this era:

> I mean to me, I know what good morals are. It would seem you're supposed to disregard good morals when you're living in a crazy bad world. If you're living cursed, how can you live like an angel? If you're in hell, how can you live like an angel? You're surrounded by devils and you're supposed to live like an angel. That's like suicide, you know what I'm sayin'?[49]

Tupac's life was filled with turmoil at the beginning of this era. He wanted to do what was right, but he was also surrounded by many "devils," which made it difficult for him to make the right decision. Tupac felt the weight of the world on him and his music reflected that burden too.

During this era we begin to see how Tupac's life was to be remembered after he was gone: as a martyr and saint. Tupac's martyrdom began the day he went to prison. For many, it was then that he was seen as someone who was being persecuted while remaining innocent. This was still overshadowed by his "outlaw" era, and his message of peace and unity was hidden under headlines such as "rapist," "cop killer," "sexist," and even "molester."

Still, through all this, we begin to see Tupac's ability to survive and his tenacious attitude to persevere through different life trials, even though Tupac's image was being tarnished and he was a public spectacle. Tupac managed to release another multi-platinum album *All Eyez on Me*. This album depicted the struggles that existed within Tupac. Tupac made it clear that only God would judge him:

> Perhaps I was blind to the facts, stabbed in the back
> I couldn't trust my own homies just a bunch a dirty rats

49. From an interview in Lazin, *Tupac: Resurrection*.

Will I, succeed, paranoid from the weed

Oh my Lord, tell me what I'm livin for
Everybody's droppin got me knockin on heaven's door
And all my memories, of seein brothers bleed
And everybody grieves, but still nobody sees
Recollect your thoughts don't get caught up in the mix
Cause the media is full of dirty tricks
Only God can judge me.[50]

We can see in the simple image of Figure 3 how Tupac's THUG LIFE code broke down. His message was twofold—both for the ghetto and for Black males. The idea to help Black males dated all the way back to 1991 on his *Strickly 4 My N.I.G.G.A.Z.* album. In an interview with Davey D, Tupac states, regarding that album, that his vision for the meaning of the tracks on the album was to encourage young Black males. Tupac felt as though the young Black male did not receive enough positive attention, so he was going to give them the positive attention he himself did not receive.

Figure 3 also depicts Tupac's goals for THUG LIFE. The goals were rooted in the "Military Mind" era. Social concern was Tupac's top priority. Tupac knew the only way to make a difference was to sink his soul into this cause, and that is what he did.

Tupac used his fame and fortune to help many. Frank Alexander, Tupac's favorite bodyguard and now urban youth worker, recounts the many times that Tupac made time for the children of the ghetto. Alexander also remembers when Tupac took time to spend with his paraplegic niece; that was a time when he was real busy and under a lot of pressure, but Tupac did it anyway; his THUG

50. Shakur, "Only God Can Judge Me," *All Eyez on Me.*

LIFE code stretched far beyond the stereotypical image of "thugs."

Figure 3: Tupac's THUG LIFE Code's Message

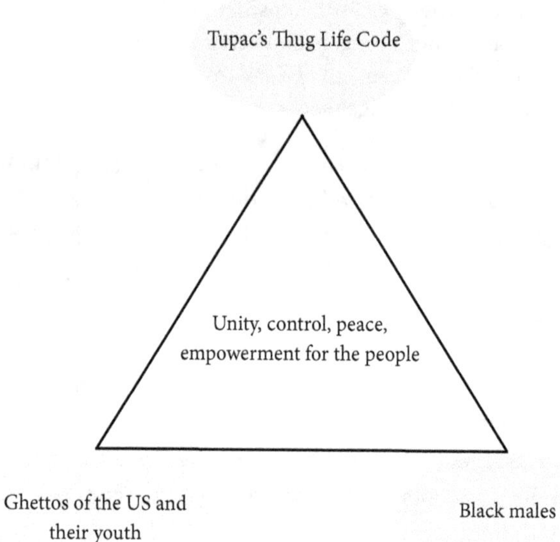

Death Row Records

There have been many accounts as to whether the move to Death Row Records was a wise move for Tupac. But at the time, he really did not have a choice. Suge Knight, Death Row's president at the time, offered to pay his million dollar bail in exchange for his signing on the label. Tupac had recently started his own label and was hoping to move into politics as well.[51] Nevertheless, despite the criticism, Tupac signed and went to Death Row Records. Tupac states:

51. It was Tupac's vision that by the year 2000 there would have been a third political party formed from Hip Hop culture. There has

> Death Row is a successful record company. It runs efficiently. Everything they've released has sold in excess of four million copies. I'm saying, why not be there? I really like everybody on the record company. I like Suge. That's my homie. I like Snoop, Dre, and Nate, and all them. I hang out with them anyway, so now it's just official. Suge ain't no gangster, man. He's chillin. Me comin' to Death Row, one of the main reasons besides Suge was Snoop. The man's got so much style. I felt like since me and Snoop's music was often coupled together when we were being criticized and when we were being praised, we getting, you know, sales and all that. So I said it would be a wise decision to team up with them and make this allegiance that much stronger, and the vibe coming out the West Coast scene that much more heavier. I'm a super power. Death Row is a super power. Let's combine super powers and ally, and really hit 'em. And that's one of the biggest combinations you can get.[52]

This was a shaping moment for Tupac. Death Row had the finances and the market to sell a lot of records. Moreover, Death Row was the king of West Coast Rap production at the time. The sound of Hip Hop during this era came from the West Coast.[53] Tupac was Death Row's crown jewel, and the fans were taking it all in. It was during this time that Tupac developed his theology for the ghetto. Songs such as "No More Pain," "Hail Mary," and "Black Jesus" were just some of the tracks that made many young

been no one to date to carry the torch for that vision.

52. This was an MTV interview when Tupac was release from prison in late 1995, interviewer unknown.

53. Arguably, currently, the sound for Hip Hop comes from what is termed "Tha Dirty South," or, in terms of genre, Trap Music.

ghetto youth feel that maybe Tupac was their own "Black Jesus." Death Row's financing and marketing helped foster and promote this image to ghettos everywhere. Now, that all said, all of the family members I interviewed told me that Tupac took a deal with the devil when he signed with Death Row and that he should have just done the time in prison so that he'd remain alive. In some sense, they were right. Tupac, toward the middle part of 1996, began to move away from Suge and Death Row. He wanted to go solo and create his own media industry that had music, film, and production. This was a large part of his future vision, along with entering politics.

This era also saw Tupac having a brutal feud with East Cost rappers Biggie and Sean "Puffy" Combs. Tupac incited that they were responsible for his shooting and that it was a setup from them. In many regards, Tupac felt as though they betrayed him and his generosity. This period saw war-like conditions emerge between the sides in music, in videos, at awards shows—it was all public and at this point in Hip Hop culture, there was no "dirty south" or "third coast," it was the East and the West. As one interviewer asked Tupac, "Who's gonna be the king of niggadom?" This was a difficult question though, because at the time Tupac and Biggie represented the two largest acts in Rap music. Many said Tupac was paranoid near the end of his life. This was not true. In what is believed to be a summer interview in 1996, Tupac discussed that he had been receiving multiple death threats, friends he once thought were close were now turning into enemies, and that there was a lot of pressure on him to leave Death Row and to create a Hip Hop political candidate. Tupac reveals the stress of fame and the struggle to be a leader at the age of twenty-five. The latter part of his life saw Tupac both as a visionary and with tremendous pressure upon his life. His pursuits in trying to create a social justice ethic for the 'hood was amazing.' Tupac made gains in uniting gangs, creating a street code, and establishing a direction for Black and Latinx youth that no politician or pastor had done. Some still say this was a large part of why he was killed.

While there have been several independent investigations into the murder of Tupac, there have been no substantial leads in his murder. Some suggest that Suge had a part in the murder since Tupac was actually considering leaving Death Row and because Suge was sitting less than a foot from Tupac when he was shot and did not endure any gunshot wounds. Still, others say it was a secret plot by government agencies to have Tupac killed. Tupac was raising money for a Hip Hop political candidate to run in the 2000 election. Tupac wanted someone from the Hip Hop context to represent the "lost tribes" he said needed representation (Armenians, Latinx, Pan Africans in the US). Some even say Tupac had figured out the illuminati and was killed for that. Tupac's death remains a mystery.

I Wonder If Heaven Got a Ghetto

In the song "I Wonder If Heaven Got a Ghetto," Tupac makes it clear that things are hard, and that even he struggles with hope and a vision for a better tomorrow. Tupac, and several of his homies, rap on the track about a heaven that can handle them. For Tupac, and many other young urbanites, the image of Jesus and of heaven has not been one that could actually handle their sin. Most of the imagery that they receive about heaven is one that can only handle the proper, secure, honest, pure, and righteous person. But Tupac challenged this view to say everyone has, in fact, sinned, so how could heaven only be for the "holy" and "righteous" person?

> Here on Earth, tell me what's a black life worth
> A bottle of juice is no excuse, the truth hurts
> And even when you take the shit
> Move counties get a lawyer you can shake the shit
> Ask Rodney, LaTasha, and many more
> It's been goin on for years, there's plenty more
> When they ask me, when will the violence cease?
> When your troops stop shootin niggaz down in the street.[54]

In this verse, Tupac explains some of the issues that urbanites have to dwell in. He entreats that no one judges him when he "loots." He "loots" because he has to; much like the people in New Orleans had to after no help came for over a week. "Word to God" is a Rap liturgical point that says God is the "man" and that God deserves all respect. Tupac is the messenger and participant in this particular track and gives the listener firsthand information about what is happening, while encouraging the people to hold on, much like Jesus did in John 15:18–27, to a brighter tomorrow rooted in heaven.

September 13, 1996

On the night of September 7, 1996, while driving with Suge Knight en route to Club 666, Tupac was shot four times in the chest by an assailant in a white Cadillac. Tupac was rushed to University Medical Hospital and underwent surgery, including the removal of his right lung. After six

54. Shakur, "I Wonder If Heaven Got a Ghetto?" *R U Still Down.*

days in critical condition, Tupac was pronounced dead at 4:03 p.m. He was only twenty-five years old.

This was the day the world stopped for many. Hip Hop artist after Hip Hop artist discussed the deep pain and mourning they went through in the days following Tupac's death. In fact, the entire six days that Tupac was in the hospital, legions of fans waited outside to gather any passing news regarding Tupac.

Tupac's fans were devastated with the news of his death. Further, not just those in the "ghetto" and "Hip Hoppers" mourned Tupac's passing. People like Tony Danza, Madonna, Jasmine Guy, Jada Pinkett-Smith, and James Belushi were among some of the many celebrities who loved Tupac. Tupac had etched his mark in American pop culture. But more importantly, he had carved his mark in the cultural continuum of Hip Hop culture. His death only raised his spiritual, thug, immortal, and Christ-like image even higher. Today, there are scores of fans who still believe he is alive, including that he might be alive on some remote island.

Tupac symbolized a generation's anger, hope, love, hate, despair, and marginality. When Tupac died, it meant that they too could die. This explains why there are still so many people who hold on to the fact that he is alive; they do not want him to die because that would mean they too are vulnerable to death. And it would mean that once again a Black leader was taken out.

This chapter should've given you a solid overview of who Tupac was. What I'd like to do next is give you a theological construct of who Tupac is today and his impact not just at the level of Hip Hop culture, but on a global level. Yeah, he was that big. And he continues to sell records . . . wow. Okay, let's dig in more!

3

A Tupacian Theological Gospel

If I were to have read the title of this chapter twenty-five years ago, I would have thrown this book into an open fire with salt to exercise those demons out. I was just that fundamentalist. The world was binary, good and evil. Nothing else. Life was a rhythmic series of church, prayer, casting judgment on the "lost," and reading my Bible, not to develop knowledge or grow closer to God, but to argue and win against those who would dare say anything contrary to my beliefs. Tupac, of course, was as secular as they came. So, of course, there was nothing he or anyone else like him, in their worldly selves, could teach me. Was I arrogant or what? But that's where a lot of religious folks are right now. Maybe even you, reading this right now, still have doubts about a "secular" person being able to theologize. I get it. It took me finally thinking for myself, asking some difficult questions, and getting married to someone my community considered "outside the faith" to really hit a space that had my theological highway of answers and easy exits finally run out of pavement and had me face the complexity and ambiguous nature of life; that's when I truly believe my spiritual journey began. It was when I faced hardship and a complete excommunication from what I had assumed was a solid life-long community that I realized, "hmm, maybe this thing of life is much more complicated than I had ever imagined." Yup. It is. But that journey was difficult and wrought with doubt, mystery, and shame at certain points. I had to face my true self and see things where I really was. Graduate school helped, a PhD gave me tools, but what was truly the game changer was the painful process of growth, which also involved therapy and dealing with my own demons—that I threw salt on.

Tupac played a role in the healing process that continues for me to this day. I am constantly learning from someone who saw God in and from the margins; from the oppressed; from the lynching tree; from the 'hood; from the corners no on looked in; from the beauty of struggle and pain. Tupac has not only aided me in my own theological pursuits, but countless others, especially those willing to push past colonized Christian ecclesiology and desire a journey that locates itself at the intersections of the sacred, secular, and profane. So, this chapter examines that intersection and attempts to look at Tupac as one would some type of European theologian. My hope here is that what we have built up in the previous chapters will now culminate in this one as we look directly at where my own research and engagement with Pac has led me.

Situating Tupac in the Post-Soul Context

To begin, we must situate four terms for Tupac and the post-soul context. First, *post-soul* in the macro sense of an entire culture differs somewhat from micro post-soul as applied to Tupac as a singular individual. Tupac, as this chapter will argue, is a post-soul personification of the rejection of norms, hegemonic authority, and dominant religious structures that inhibit community building.[1] So, the post-soul is the era that began in the late 1960s and early 1970s and that rejected dominant structures, systems, and meta-narratives which tended to exclude ethnic minorities and particularly the 'hood. The post-soul era rejects linear functional mantras[2] and embraces communal approaches to life, love, and God. The post-soul context was formed in the cocoon of a social shift that broke open the dam to the questioning of authority, challenging the status quo, asserting one's self identity in the public sphere, and questioning group leaders.[3] The post-soul embodies a more urban, ethnic minority, Hip Hop worldview. Therefore, while still recognizing the societal shift that occurred during those years, the post-soul is a more multicultural/ethnic approach to postmodernity and the issues it raises.[4]

1. Alper, "Making Sense Out of Postmodern Music?"; Bauman, "Postmodern Religion?"; Cox, *Religion in the Secular City*; Cupitt, "Post-Christianity."

2. Sequential based reasoning, linear worldviews (first this, then that, lastly this, etc.), and simplistic answers.

3. As discussed in George, *Hiphop America*; Hodge, *Soul of Hip Hop*; Neal, "Sold Out on Soul"; Neal, *What the Music Said*; Neal, *Soul Babies*; Pinn, *Black Church*; Pinn, *Embodiment and the New Shape of Black Theology*.

4. For example, books such as Best and Kellner, *Postmodern Theory*, fall short of mentioning the social, religious, and cultural shift that the civil rights movement brought to the American public sphere. Moreover, Betts, *History of Popular Culture*, does not mention—even briefly—the contributions of Hip Hop and Rap moguls. In the work of Lash, "Postmodernism as Humanism?"; and Lash, *Sociology of Postmodernism*; Gil Scott-Heron, Ray Charles, and even the television show *Fresh Prince of Bel-Air* were never mentioned in the literature. While each of these represent major changes and social shifts, they were not engaged. The post-soul, as argued in chapter 1, is therefore a parallel conceptual framework including those excluded voices and creating space for artists like Tupac. Tupac asserted time after time that race played a role in the historical discourse of people,

Second, post-soul *theology* is the theology of the post-soul context. Its vernacular prioritizes a connection with a God of the oppressed and disenfranchised. Post-soul theology seeks to better understand God in the profane, the blasphemous, and the irreverent. Moreover, it makes God accessible to humans in a multiethnic and inclusive way while still recognizing the atrocities committed in the name of religion.[5]

Third, many renowned evangelical theologians have argued that we live in a "secular" culture. However, within the post-soul context, *spirituality* makes its reemergence and seeks to discover God in the ordinary. This pathway is foreign to traditional methodologies of salvation. The neo-secular is a mixture of sacred and profane spiritual journeys pursuing God in a space outside traditional forms of worship.

Fourth, *neo-sacred* is rooted in the post-soul theological context. This sacred space embodies city corners, alleyways, club rooms, cocktail lounges, and spaces/places that are extraneous to many who call themselves "Christian." The neo-sacred is Tupac's message to the pimps, the hookers, the thugs, the niggas, those overlooked by society, missionaries, and many churchgoers. The neo-sacred is concerned with finding God in the post-soul socio-ecological landscape and making God accessible for all.

Tupac was more than just a fad or an "estranged artist." He had a mission and message that few are able to embrace. The cost is high: your life. Tupac saw life and culture beyond the routine and ordinary; he approached life full of passion, rage, anger, love, thoughtfulness, and even carelessness. He was the product of a post-soul society that

---

and the post-soul aids in filling that void.

5. Hodge, "No Church in the Wild."

had been groomed on the ambiguous consumer culture of the 1980s.[6] In this consumer culture, Tupac became a type of popular critical pundit for the Hip Hop community, which was established early on in Hip Hop culture in its critique of US social structures—particularly religion and economics. He was a by-product of the post-revolutionary Black spirit alive in the early 1970s.[7] He was the voice of the ghetto/'hood, marginalized, oppressed, and downtrodden,[8] connecting God to a people who would never imagine gracing the pristine hallways of a church. He related God, culture, Hip Hop, life, pain, and even "sin" to Jesus, and forced the listener to deal with those issues while offering an accessible pathway and access to a God that was not marred with a blonde-haired, blue-eyed embodiment of perfection. Tupac's God was the God of the 'hood. As Cheryl Kirk-Duggan so eloquently states of Tupac, "Amid his deep hurt and alienation, he often expressed profound religious sensibilities—a kind of street spirituality that invokes traditional faith categories [and] ranging from irony and sarcasm to humility and sincerity, aware of the life and death issues that people face daily on the street."[9]

Tupac was also the product of his mother's, Afeni Shakur's, upbringing in the Black church

6. Covert, "Consumption and Citizenship."

7. See also Pinn, *Black Church*, in which he discusses the effects of the civil rights movement, post-soul creations, and post-revolutionary elements for the Black church and Black theology.

8. While this was Tupac's main audience, there have been numerous suburban, wealthy, White people who connected with Tupac's message simply because they themselves were marginalized, oppressed, and/or downtrodden by parents and/or other structural forces similar to that of the urban poor.

9. Kirk-Duggan, "Theo-Poetic Theological Ethics," 214.

framework—which, as previously stated in chapter 1, was connected to protest and praise. Afeni gave Tupac his foundation and provided a theological foundation for his later life. Afeni helped create in Tupac a key theological concept in ethnic cohesion as evidenced in Afrocentric thinking and theologizing. This gave Tupac the context in which to create and think about not just the Missio Dei in his own life, but also for the community. Tupac continually emphasized that work needed to be done in order to benefit the community; if it did not benefit the community, it was not worth the work.

Tupac wove a strand of theological ontology through the intersections of the sacred, secular, and the profane; a place where Tupac resided daily and where he found a lot of meaning pursuing the numinous. It was a space outside the traditional environment of "church" and a space for the "thugs," the "niggas," and the "'hood rats." Tupac was, in a matter of speaking, creating a neo-sacred theology,[10] which he in turn was asserting as a contextualized spirituality of and for the urban post-soul community. Tupac gave the broader American media outlets a view into "the 'hood" and said that there is much to engage with and learn from, theologically speaking, at the intersections of the sacred, profane, and secular and within what seems apparently blasphemous.[11]

10. This term is used to define the intersection of the profane and the sacred, a space that has elements of both deity and sin while yet pointing to divine edification in the midst of chaos, pain, blasphemy, and irreverence.

11. This takes up the argument begun by Benjamín Valentín in regards to sketching cultural theology and the importance of relevant cultural figures within a theological space. While Valentín argues for a Latinx cultural theology, I would argue that Tupac is part of that process even though he was African American. And that many young Latinos in particular saw Tupac as part of their own cultural

For Tupac, a new type of theological discourse was needed in the face of severe economic, social, and political disparities. For example, in one of his first songs, "Panther Power," Tupac bellows:

> As real as it seems the American Dream
> Ain't nothing but another calculated scheme
> To get us locked up shot up back in chains
> To deny us of the future rob our names
> Kept my history of mystery but now I see
> The American Dream wasn't meant for me
> Cause lady liberty is a hypocrite she lied to me.[12]

Tupac calls out the very fabric of the "American Dream" (home ownership, being educated, affordable health care, and day care)[13] and challenges its apparent mythology for the ghetto poor. Where is God in all of this? Where is justice for those who do not live the commercialized embodiment of "the good life"? Tupac asserts the neo-sacred within this pain and disillusionment in a song titled "Lord Knows":

> I smoke a blunt to take the pain out

---

geography. For instance, Valentín asserts that Latino youth realize that culture matters. There are more ways in which they are being oppressed and which affect Latino lives than simply economic factors: cultural imperialism, racism, sexism. Tupac covered these in his music and felt connected to this type of critical cultural discourse from him. See Valentín, "Tracings," 39–40.

12. Shakur, "Panther Power," *The Lost Tapes*.

13. These four "American Dream" taxonomies are what Block et al., "Compassion Gap," describe as the four main constructs of the "American Dream," and how the exponential increase in all four of those areas between 1973 and 2003 have almost eliminated the middle class. For Tupac, and many other Black scholars, the poor, the ghetto, and African Americans are at the bottom of this avalanche of misery. These are also building blocks for Western Evangelical Christianity and used as part of Christian exceptionalism.

And if I wasn't high, I'd probably try to blow
 my brains out
I'm hopeless, they shoulda killed me as a baby
And now they got me trapped in the storm, I'm goin
 crazy
Forgive me; they wanna see me in my casket
and if I don't blast I'll be the victim of them bastards
I'm losin hope, they got me stressin, can the Lord
 forgive me
Got the spirit of a thug in me.[14]

At the same time, Tupac realizes that this is not the way life was supposed to be. He is fully aware that God has not intended people to behave in an inhumane fashion. He calls out to God in a post-soul style, decrying his lifestyle:

Fuck the friendships, I ride alone
Destination Death Row, finally found a home
Plus all my homies wanna die, call it euthanasia
Dear Lord, look how sick this ghetto made us, sincerely
yours I'm a thug, the product of a broken home.[15]

In these lyrics, Tupac "does what he has to" in order to survive within these types of injustices, while still asking the poignant theological questions of God in the face of suffering. Tupac presents a voice to engage culture, deal with conflict, create cohesive narrative, generate community, dispel the traditional powers, and call people to a different level of engagement with God. Cheryl Kirk-Duggan would say that "like James Baldwin, Shakur confronted black suffering with a moral ire."[16] For those who would argue that this type of approach to life is vile, immoral, and "sinful," Tupac would reply that only God can judge him:

14. Shakur, "Lord Knows," *Me Against The World.*

15. Shakur, "Letter to the President," *Still I Rise.*

16. Kirk-Duggan, "Theo-Poetic Theological Ethics," 219.

Oh my Lord, tell me what I'm livin for
Everybody's droppin got me knockin on heaven's door
And all my memories, of seein brothers bleed
And everybody grieves, but still nobody sees
Recollect your thoughts don't get caught up in the mix
Cause the media is full of dirty tricks
Only God can judge me.[17]

Blues music had a similar sense. Contextual, relevant, gritty, and with reflections of Black lives in the White supremacist South, the blues were dismissed as evil, sinful, and altogether vile by many White conservatives and religious Blacks. Teresa Reed reminds us that "blues singing was associated with the brothel, the juke joint, and the dregs of black-American society."[18] Still, despite the stench of "sin," Reed argues that the "religious commentary is salient in the blues text. . . . These lyrics treat religion in a way that yields two important kinds of information: integration of secular thought with sacred and . . . the postbellum shift in black-American religious consciousness."[19] Tupac's music is merely a continuation of this postbellum shift, now with Rap music.[20]

A great example of part of this shift came in the late 1960s and early 1970s, when a heated debate was brewing that Black theology had no relevance and merely reflected an "angry" and "hateful" message from Blacks.[21] Black theologian Herbert Edwards, in response to claims from some White theologians that Black theology was not a valid theological approach, argued that Black theology

17. Shakur, "Only God Can Judge Me," *All Eyez On Me*, disc 1.

18. Reed, *Holy Profane*, 39.

19. Reed, *Holy Profane*, 39–40.

20. Hodge, *Soul of Hip Hop*.

21. e.g., Cone, *Black Theology and Black Power*.

provided contextualization, a voice, and offered a way for those who had previously been either dismissed by White evangelicals or forcibly assimilated to their tradition. Tupac begins to create such a Black theological space.[22]

Tupac argues the inadequacy of the previous and existing theologies for the present crisis: poverty, recidivism rates for young urban males, racism, and classism. Tupac never once questioned, blasphemed, or cursed the name of God or Jesus. What Tupac did do was to call out religious officials, traditionalized churches (churches practicing hyper-traditionalism and adherence to the "letter of the law"), conventional forms of religion, irrelevant theologies, and current methods of evangelism.

Tupac was not a trained theologian, pastor, or evangelist in the way one would recognize from the formal rigor of the seminary.[23] Tupac did not have the eloquence of a T. D. Jakes or the patois of a Baptist preacher. Still, Tupac was able to connect God to the streets and give those who had never heard of God a vision for what their life could be like. For Tupac, and others like him, lacking formal seminary training never disqualified him, or others, from doing "God's work." Still, Tupac never really came to any solid conclusions about a theology of the 'hood. He

22. Edwards, while discussing Black theology, argues that in order for theologies to have a concrete basis they must prove the inadequacy of the preceding theologies, establish and prove their own adequacy for the present, and must establish continuity with the primordial, normative expressions of the faith. See Edwards, "Black Theology," 46–47.

23. In my 2008 research, nineteen of the twenty interviewees stated that Tupac was their "pastor" and had a connection to theology. They told me that Tupac was a prophet because of the way he could interpret theological matters and make it "clear" for them. See Hodge, *Soul of Hip Hop*.

began the discussion, but because of his early death, he never finished the mantra of a ghetto Gospel.

> We probably in Hell already, our dumb asses not
> knowin
> Everybody kissin ass to go to heaven ain't goin
> Put my soul on it, I'm fightin devil niggaz daily
> Plus the media be crucifying brothers severely.[24]

This aptly-titled song "Blasphemy" was a rejection of a form of Black theology that places the pastor at the center of the church, creates a pious stature for him (and it typically is a him), and discourages honest questions and doubts from emerging within the congregation.[25] Tupac not only challenges but shatters the status quo by placing context and reality into his message within this song. He further states:

> The preacher want me buried why? Cause I know
> he a liar
> Have you ever seen a crackhead, that's eternal fire
> Why you got these kids minds, thinkin that they evil
> while the preacher bein richer you say honor God's
> people
> Should we cry, when the Pope die, my request
> We should cry if they cried when we buried Malcolm X
> Mama tell me am I wrong, is God just another cop
> waitin to beat my ass if I don't go pop?[26]

24. Shakur, "Blasphemy," *The Don Killuminati: The 7 Day Theory* (1996).

25. Pinn, *Embodiment and the New Shape of Black Theology*.

26. In this verse we can also see Tupac connecting with mainstream theological thought by asking the serious questions of God. In other words, is God just another White, conservative Republican, wanting me to fit in and wear suits and ties like I've been told and have seen? Is there a place for the real nigga and thug in heaven?

Tupac continues shattering the status quo of "nice" theological answers by offering up metaphorical comparisons:

> They ask us why we mutilate each other like we do
> They wonder why we hold such little worth
> for human life
> Facing all this drama
> To ask us why we turn from bad to worse is to ignore
> from which we came
> You see, you wouldn't ask why the rose that grew from
> the concrete had
> damaged petals
> On the contrary, we would all celebrate its tenacity
> We would all love its will to reach the sun
> Well, we are the roses
> This is the concrete
> And these are my damaged petals
> Don't ask me why
> Thank God, nigga
> Ask me how.[27]

In one of his greatest theological songs, "So Many Tears," Tupac pushes past the "milk" theology, described by Paul in 1 Corinthians 3:2, and into a "solid food" theological stance on life:

> Now that I'm strugglin in this business, by any means
> Label me greedy gettin green, but seldom seen
> And fuck the world cause I'm cursed, I'm havin visions
> of leavin here in a hearse, God can you feel me?
> Take me away from all the pressure, and all the pain
> Show me some happiness again, I'm goin blind
> I spend my time in this cell, ain't livin well
> I know my destiny is Hell, where did I fail?
> My life is in denial, and when I die,
> baptized in eternal fire I'll shed so many tears

27. Shakur, "Mama Just a Little Girl" *Better Dayz*, disc 1.

Lord, I suffered through the years, and shed so many tears.[28]

The post-soul context requires one to disembody and deconstruct current theological mantras that continually hold up tradition. Pain, injustice, and racism force the post-soulist to look beyond the "standard" and ask God for more. Simplistic answers are rejected and despised: it gets God off the hook too easily to say "just pray about it,"[29] and in times of pain and injustice, everything needs to be on the hook, including God. The procedure is quite simple: have a conversation with God, be real, and do not be afraid to use strong language to describe your pain—a crucial element of a missiology at the intersections of the sacred, profane, and secular:

Was it my fault papa didn't plan it out
Broke out left me to be the man of the house
I couldn't take it, had to make a profit
Down the block, got a glock, and I clock grip
Makin G's was my mission
Movin enough of this shit to get my mama out the kitchen and
why must I sock a fella, just to live large like Rockefeller
First you didn't give a fuck, but you're learnin now
If you don't respect the town then we'll burn you down
God damn it's a motherfuckin' riot

I see no changes, all I see is racist faces
Misplaced hate makes disgrace to races

28 Shakur, "So Many Tears," *Me Against the World.*

29. Pinn, *Why Lord?*, describes this type of theological process as nitty gritty hermeneutics, pushing past the basics of theology and into the depths of life to ask God "tougher questions." Acceptance of pain is put into context and the hermeneutic moves into the "nitty gritty" of life.

We under I wonder what it take to make this
one better place, let's erase the wait state
Take the evil out the people they'll be acting right
Cause both black and white are smokin crack tonight
And only time we deal is when we kill each other
It takes skill to be real, time to heal each other
Pull a trigger kill a nigger he's a hero
Mo' nigga mo' nigga mo' niggaz
I'd rather be dead than a po' nigga
Let the Lord judge the criminals
If I die, I wonder if heaven got a ghetto.[30]

For Tupac, the goal was to create a manner in which a portion of society who had been forgotten, those living in urban enclaves, could still be human and have meaning. In his song "Searching for Black Jesuz," Tupac and the Outlawz search for a deity that can relate to them, one who "smokes like we smoke, drink like we drink."[31] In the song "Picture Me Rolling" Tupac questions whether or not God can forgive him as he asks, "Will God forgive me for all the dirt a nigga did to feed his kids?"[32] In this neo-sacred element, Tupac begins to ask the long-standing theological question: what does forgiveness really look like for sinners?

For the urban post-soulist, this process of searching for God in the mystery, the hurt, the pain, and then finding God in that heinous mixture is a welcome breath of fresh air compared to the avoidance and three-point sermons that so much of evangelical theology has become. It is the heart of dialogue and the very place God is experienced. In fact, almost anyone who has experienced deep loss and pain in which God's hand felt far can relate. For example, "White

30. Lyrics taken from throughout the song "I Wonder If Heaven Got a Ghetto," *R U Still Down,* disc 1.

31. Tupac and The Outlawz,"Black Jesus," *Still I Rise.*

32. Tupac interview with *Vibe Magazine*, approximately 1995.

Man's World" combines Tupac's request for heavenly favor and reprisal in a process similar to the Psalms: "God bless me please. . . . Making my enemies bleed."[33] Within those statements much more is at work—a fundamental attempt to make God accessible in a social structure that has been forgotten and left for dead.

More of the neo-sacred and post-soul theology arises in songs such as "Hail Mary." The song suggests a liturgical prayer, beseeching listeners to follow God and to "follow me; eat my flesh."[34] While it might appear that Tupac is asking his listeners to see him as "God," in fact Tupac was acting as a type of pastoral go-between. In several interviews from the early 1990s, he made reference to people in the 'hood not always having a clear path to God, and that in that absence of such a path, if he was the only pathway, then he'd gladly take up that mantle.[35] Tupac made it clear he was not God or Jesus, but merely a conduit and a beacon to a contextualized Jesuz.[36]

Tupac fills part of the vacancy for those who doubt. In the song "Po Nigga Blues," Tupac poses a question to

33. Shakur, "White Man's World," *Makaveli-Don Killuminati: The 7-Day Theory*.

34. Shakur, "Hail Mary," *Makaveli-Don Killuminati: The 7-Day Theory*.

35. Tupac interview with *Vibe Magazine*, approximately 1995.

36. Note the letter S has been dropped to demonstrate the contextualization of the Christ figure for the ghetto. And the letter Z at the end of Jesus' name was added to give a portrait of a Jesus that could sympathize and connect with a people that were downtrodden and broken. The letter Z is consistent with Hip Hop's vernacular to change words and phrases to fit the context and annunciation of words for a Hip Hop community. The Z also represented a Jesus who was not only "above" in theological discussions, but also "below" in reachable form. The Z gives new dimensions to the portrait of Christ and validates the struggles, life, narrative, and spirituality for many Hip Hoppers. Hodge, *Soul of Hip Hop*, chapter 6.

God that oozes with spiritual doubt: "I wonder if the Lord ever heard of me, huh, I need loot, so I'm doin' what I do."[37] In other words, will God really forgive me when I am practicing socially unapproved standards of living? Dyson reminds us that "Tupac's religious ideas were complex and unorthodox, perhaps even contradictory, though that would not make him unique among his believers."[38] Part of that vacancy felt in the 'hood also comes with images of heaven: streets of gold, mansions, pearly gates, and a God who is "perfect"—these may be too much for the person living on streets riddled with potholes, in project housing, around broken gates, and with White racist images of God. Paulo Freire states that within situations of oppression, the main goal of the oppressed should be to "liberate themselves from their oppressor."[39] Tupac in his own way was helping to create that pathway for liberation.[40]

Tupac had a post-soul theological gospel message for his fans, community, and society, embodying both the sacred and the profane. Tupac owned a lot of his own "sins" and shortcomings, which, in post-soul contexts, creates a kind of transparency and authenticity. His listeners

37. Shakur, "Po Nigga Blues," *Loyal to the Game.*

38. Dyson, *Holler If You Hear Me*, 204.

39. Freire, *Pedagogy of the Oppressed*, 28.

40. It is interesting to note that within my interviews, a theme of liberation from traditional church arose from the interviewees. "To move away from," "get out from under," and "move out" were all phrases from respondents, when asked, "How has Tupac's music, poetry, and spirituality affected you theologically?" These phrases were part of a larger discussion on how contemporary religion had become corrupted and lost its "edge" in life. Whether or not race was a factor in this response was not analyzed. This would be something for further study, but there is a clear implication here that the interviewees felt they needed to move out from their current theological situation and that Tupac helped them to do just that.

could identify with a marred, scarred, profanity-ridden, and broken ghetto "preacher." Within that profanity, an attempt to create honest communication between God and humankind is at work. Tupac and E. D. I. contend, in the song "The Uppercut," that "I'm a product of the pimp, the pusher, and the reverend. . . . We all lost souls trying to find our way to heaven."[41] What would a missiology look like if it began with that premise? How might we then entreat the BLM movement in the Christian church?

Dyson asserts that "Tupac aimed to enhance awareness of the divine, of spiritual reality, by means of challenging orthodox beliefs and traditional religious practices."[42] Tupac's "gospel," in essence, was a mature one that sought to better apprehend God in the core of a world gone askew—critical to a theology that pursues decolonizing itself.

Tupac's "Good News"

Tupac's "good news," conversely, about life in a post-soul context, is a type of "indecent theology" in the same hue as Marcella Althaus-Reid's *Indecent Theology: Theological Perversions in Sex, Gender, and Politics.*[43] As grand narratives of God have collapsed in mainstream society, creating parallel narratives that are contextual and relatable are crucial and desired by post-soulists. Tupac's gospel, at its core, seeks to give marginalized urban dwellers (and

41. Tupac, "The Uppercut," *Loyal to the Game.*

42. Dyson, *Holler If You Hear Me*, 204.

43. See Althaus-Reid, *Indecent Theology*, as she discusses an "indecent" approach to theology by questioning the authority figures within that religious structure and allowing new voices to emerge (in her case, a feminist perspective on religion).

disenfranchised Whites for that matter) a voice to God and a place for meaning in unbearable conditions. For Tupac, it is about the tension of grappling with depression, dead friends, racism, and keeping God in focus through all of that. Tupac is an indirect "theologian," bringing a neo-secular message of God's love to the people and contextualizing epistemological processes—in other words, constructing a new knowledge set of life for a generation raised in the crack cocaine milieu. Jamal Joseph notes that Tupac had a huge heart for people to understand a better way of living, to know positive role models, and to be critical thinkers.[44] Tupac is a contradiction within a saintly modality—in other words, while Tupac had saintly attributes, he was also raw, uncut, and indecent in his approach to theology. Yet, he was able to communicate authentically the struggles of his own life, while still invoking the spirit of Jesus in protest. Thus, there are three gospel messages within both their works: the gospel of hold on, the gospel of keeping ya head up, and the gospel of heaven having a ghetto.

First, the gospel of hold on encourages those who have given up or are about to give up on life or other people.[45] Tupac encourages his listener to see that there is hope for a brighter tomorrow:

> God
> When I was alone, and had nothing
> I asked for a friend to help me bear the pain
> No one came, except God
> When I needed a breath to rise, from my sleep
> No one could help me . . . except God
> When all I saw was sadness, and I needed answers
> No one heard me, except God

44. Jospeh, *Tupac Shakur*, 16–23.

45. E.g., Iverem, "Politics of 'Fuck It.'"

So when I'm asked . . . who I give my unconditional
 love to?
I look for no other name, except God.[46]

In this poem, entitled "God," Tupac calls out to God and asks for a conduit. He finds it in the midst of hurt. James Cone calls this type of process "revelation" and argues, "For black theology, revelation is not just a past event or a contemporary event in which it is difficult to recognize the activity of God. Revelation is a black event."[47] In this poem, Tupac takes on the revelation and looks for no one else but God.

In the song "So Many Tears,"[48] Tupac begs God not to forget a nigga, "Lord I suffered through the years and shed so many tears . . . dear God please let me in."[49] There is a paradoxical optimism in the midst of extreme pain, hurt, despair, and violence.[50] Tupac calls the person to seek a better way and higher level of understanding.

The gospel of keeping your head up was a frequent theme in Tupac's discourse. Howard Thurman stated that one of the ingenuities of Black slave culture was the ability

46. Shakur, read by Rev. Run, "God," *The Rose That Grew From Concrete Vol. 1.*

47. Cone, *Black Theology of Liberation*, 30.

48. Shakur, "So Many Tears," *Me Against the World.*

49. This mindset is no different than what slaves had to deal with and their vision that God would eventually help them. Luke Powery asserts that the spirit of lament is combined with celebration and that they go hand in hand. See Powery, *Spirit Speech.*

50. This ideology connects with a concept that Rudolf Otto calls "The Mysterium Tremendum." See Otto, *Idea of the Holy*, 12–24. The mysteriousness of what God did in spite of an appalling situation. For Otto, this meant that "a God comprehended is no God" (25). In other words, holding on does not always mean that it will make sense or will even "feel right." This was an area for Tupac that helped him deal with the bigger picture of sin and the brokenness of humankind.

to not diminish hopes, dreams, or visions to immediate experience. The immediate experience may by hurtful, may be problematic, may be nefarious, may even be abusive but one must foster, encourage, manifest, and manage the future vision that allows one to escape the immediate consequences of despair. Hopelessness occurs when one has the inability to imagine a different future.[51] In this gospel Tupac is essentially making sense of immediate pain and suffering. Tupac would say, "Yes, I'm holding on, but where do I look?"

Tupac wanted his fans to know that the act of "keeping ya head up" was not done in vain. In the face of extreme opposition and hurt, there was still a way to move forward. Even when things seemed as though they could not get any better, Tupac would tell his fans that there was a better way. Life did not end on the experience of the immediate event; one's errors and successes were not necessarily their defining moments.[52]

> If I upset you don't stress, never forget
> That God isn't finished with me yet
> I feel his hand on my brain
> When I write rhymes I go blind and let the Lord do his thang
> But am I less holy?
> Cause I chose to puff a blunt, and drink a beer with my homies
> Before we find world peace
> We gotta find peace and end the war in the streets, my ghetto gospel.[53]

51. Thurman, *Jesus and the Disinherited.*

52. Cone, *Black Theology and Black Power*; Master P, Kane and Abel, "Black Jesus," *The 7 Sins.*

53. Shakur, "Ghetto Gospel," *Loyal to the Game.*

Tupac attempted to bring a pragmatic type of hope for the listener through his music instead of traditional hymns. Tupac replaced them with the THUG LIFE mantra and his message of encouragement in hard times.[54]

Regarding the authority of what is from God and what is not, Dyson writes:

> Countless sacred narratives are hardly distinguishable from contemporary rap. . . . The prophet Jeremiah belched despair from the belly of his relentless pessimism. And the Psalms are full of midnight and bad cheer. This is not to argue that the contrasting moral frameworks of rap and religion do not color our interpretation of their often-opposing creeds. But we must not forget that unpopular and unacceptable views are sometimes later regarded as prophetic. It is a central moral contention of Christianity that God may be disguised in the clothing—and maybe even the rap—of society's most despised members.[55]

Tupac was part of this long tradition of lament, praise, and life in the secular, or what James Cone calls the "secular spiritual."[56]

In the song "Hold Ya Head," Tupac encourages those who are in prison, in pain, and lost to hold on and keep

54. Hodge, *Heaven Has a Ghetto*, 278–84. Also, this was one of the reasons why Tupac was so calm, almost at peace, with the knowledge of his imminent death. Joseph, *Tupac Shakur*. Tupac was fully aware that life did not end here. Even though he did not have it easy and his situation was nefarious, there was a better place in heaven set for him.

55. Dyson, *Holler If You Hear Me*, 208–9.

56. Cone, "The Blues," 68–97.

that head up in times of trouble. Through weed, alcohol, and even illicit sex, a post-soul theology arises:[57]

> The weed got me tweakin in my mind, I'm thinkin
> God bless the child that can hold his own
> Indeed, enemies bleed when I hold my chrome
> Let these words be the last to my unborn seeds
> Hope to raise my young nation in this world of greed
> Currency means nothin if you still ain't free
> Money breeds jealousy, take the game from me
> I hope for better days, trouble comes naturally
> Running from authorities 'til they capture me
> And my aim is to spread mo' smiles than tears
> Utilize lessons learned from my childhood years
> Maybe Mama had it all right, rest yo' head
> Tradin conversation all night, bless the dead
> To the homies that I used to have that no longer roll
> Catch a brother at the crossroads. . .
> Plus nobody knows my soul, watchin time pass
> Through the glass of my drop-top Rolls, hold ya head![58]

In the song "Still I Rise," Tupac laments to the Lord that the struggle is almost too much to bear; pain and misery parade his life and the journey seems like it will never end. Yet, in the end, still I rise. "Tupac sounds out that in times of trouble, God is with you, so keep your head up. Even the words in that phrase, 'head up' is meant to persuade one to look unto the heavens from which our help comes."[59]

57. For those who practice moralism, they begin to look outside its confined view of what a Christian looks like. Jesus himself was considered a heretic, a blasphemer, and a profane individual for his views on spiritual matters. c.f., Jack Miles, *Christ*.

58. Shakur, "Hold Ya Head," *The Don Killuminati: The 7 Day Theory*.

59. Hodge, *Heaven Has a Ghetto*, 264.

Lastly, the gospel of heaven having a ghetto is a prolific thought in Tupac's worldview, contextualizing heaven and making it accessible for people who do not subscribe to Euro-Western theology. Tupac even calls himself the "ghetto missionary." In an interview on BET, Tupac states:

> If I can't be free, if I can't live with the same respect as the next man, then I don't wanna be here. Because God has cursed me to see what life should be like. If God had wanted me to be this person, to be happy here, he wouldn't let me feel so oppressed. He wouldn't let me feel so trampled on; you know what I'm saying? He wouldn't let me think the things I think. So, I feel like I'm doing God's work, you know what I'm saying? Just because I don't have nothing to pass around for people to put in the bucket don't mean I'm not doing God's work; I feel like I'm doing God's work. Because, these ghetto kids ain't God's children? And I don't see no missionaries coming through there. So I'm doing God's work. While Reverend Jackson do his shit up in the middle class and he go to the White House and have dinner and pray over the president, I'm up in the 'hood doing my work with my folks.[60]

Here Tupac expresses not only the divisions of class within Black society, but also within its theological walls.[61] Tupac knows it is his mission to bring a Gospel to those who have been left out and have not been invited to the anticipated heavenly party with its unspoiled clean streets. The thought then is this: if life continues according to plan, heaven will have cops waiting to "beat our ass" the minute

60. Taken from an interview on BET by Ed Gordon in 1994.

61. This is an ongoing debate and issue within Black culture and the Black church. For a further discussion see Dyson, *Is Bill Cosby Right?*; Lincoln and Mamiya, *Black Church*; Pinn, *Black Church*.

we walk through the gates. Therefore, Tupac decided to ask the question, Does heaven have a ghetto? Can I be accepted in this realm that has continually told me I am neither worthy nor acceptable? Can I be taken for my own worth as I am, or do I have to enter through the back so as not to disturb the residents nor mar the fine linen?

The great writer, mystic, and theologian Howard Thurman asks the relevant and almost irreligious question regarding religion and its message to the poor and disheveled: "What does our religion say to them?"[62] Thurman's challenge says:

> I can count on the fingers of one hand the number of times that I have heard a sermon on the meaning of religion, on Christianity, to the man who stands with his back against the wall. It is urgent that my meaning be crystal clear. The masses of men live with their backs constantly against the wall. They are the poor, the disinherited, the dispossessed. What does our religion say to them?[63]

Tupac took the challenge and made an attempt to create a Gospel message for those poor, disinherited, and dispossessed peoples living in the urban enclaves called the ghetto; Tupac crated a transcendental space for the thug, the nigga, and the pimp to find God.[64]

62. Thurman, *Jesus and the Disinherited*, 13

63. Thurman, *Jesus and the Disinherited*, 13.

64. These types of questions create theological conundrums in contemporary evangelical theology, which echo vagueness and ambiguity regarding God's love to marginalized peoples. Therefore, the Hip Hopper, the ghetto person, and Tupac himself pose a new question: if social structures and systems have failed us, wouldn't the church and religion follow suit? Tupac could no longer sit by and accept a traditional view of Jesus or Christianity. Tupac needed a stronger theology than that, a Christ who could accept the thug and

Tupac's answer to his own question, "Does heaven got a ghetto?" is yes! However, not in the literal sense. Tupac never said that there is poverty, crime, gentrification, and homelessness in God's kingdom. The term is used figuratively, symbolically, as if to ask, "Is the gospel big enough to fit everyone who wants to fit in, and can God handle me if he really created me?" Tupac resoundingly said yes. He encouraged his audience, as a pastor would their flock, to see that there was a different image of heaven outside of a Eurocentric view and that there was room for those who did not fit in a traditional evangelical White theology.[65]

> Who's got the heart to stand beside me?
> I feel my enemies creepin up in silence
> Dark prayer, scream violence—demons all around me
> Can't even bend my knees just a lost cloud; Black Jesus
> give me a reason to survive, in this earthly hell
> Cause I swear, they tryin to break my well
> I'm on the edge lookin down at this volatile pit
> Will it matter if I cease to exist? Black Jesus.[66]

Toward a Theology of the Post-Soul Prophet

Tupac was not perfect. He was baptized in the dirty waters of marketing, social representations of Blackness,

---

the marginalized person. This was the outcry in songs like "I Wonder If Heaven Got a Ghetto?" and "Black Jesuz." These were expressions of a deeper search for God and spirituality. These were also fundamental questions of who God really is—questions that many of us ask ourselves such as are we really "saved?" Hodge, *Heaven Has a Ghetto*, 264–65.

65. This is also something I discuss at length in my chapter on engaging the theology of the profane in Hodge, *Soul Of Hip Hop*, 159–64.

66. Tupac and The Outlawz, "Black Jesus," *Still I Rise*.

stereotypes of the gangsta, the tattooed thug, and the poor Black child. He was not Jesus incarnate, nor was he the "perfect" role model for everyone. Before he left for prison, he told Jada Pinkett Smith that he wanted to quit thuggin' and give up on Rap and solely do acting.[67] However, Tupac ended up embodying the same Black male image he had fought so hard against for so long: the cyclical prison inmate, the nihilistic Black male, the paranoid pessimistic urbanite. This is troublesome and in many ways, he still used women in videos in a misogynist, hypermasculine manner; this was something that in his diaries he struggled with and wasn't sure how to get around it. These are areas that are present in the human species; contradictory values in many regards and a complex recipe of good, bad, and very ugly. Tupac was indeed that which made him so attractive for those living in a post-soul context. He represented both the good and the bad—the two sides of the coin. Tupac also gave you his sins and demanded you deal with them along with your own. Introspection was a key element to Tupac's own development, but because of his unique transparent nature, he created a space in which others were able to do the same.

It is within these conflicts that this paradox between the sacred and the profane arises—a post-soul theology with Tupac in the middle. Tupac embodied both sin and deity; a trait that is a much-needed direction in Christian theology in the twenty-first century. Yet, within this contradiction, there is both good and evil, sin and salvation, dirt and cleanliness all at work and having the ability to create a fuller faith, one that is honest about both the "good" and the "bad." This is the human struggle. Tupac, in this sense, was no different than Paul. While Tupac knew

67. Dyson, *Holler If You Hear Me*, 215–16.

what was right/how to do the right thing, he did not do it because the flesh was weak (Romans 7:7–24). Still, within that weakness, he sought space to find God and Jesuz. This is a large part of post-soul theology. Tupac gives us this gospel and lets us know that he is not the way; he is only pointing the way to Jesuz from a Hip Hop cultural context.[68]

Wilbert Shenk, a Mennonite theologian, echoes this sentiment,

> When the church lives in conscious response to the reign of God, its life is governed by only one criterion. Indeed, the power of the church's witness depends on the extent to which God's kingdom defines and shapes that witness. When the church attempts to make its ministry relevant by rendering "respectable" service, it has adopted an alien criterion and it becomes merely mundane.[69]

Tupac presents a post-soul theology that I break down into five parts:

1. He lived a life transparent and in relation to his own issues/problems. In other words, he is able to truly identify with sin, shortcomings, inadequacies, and deficiencies. He does not run from them nor hide them. As humans, this is our reality. As Christians, this is our reality. Theologically, those who are able to come "as is" will be much more engageable. Tupac insisted that people not reduce their hopes, dreams, and visions to the level of the event. For someone

68. This connects to John the Baptist in John 1:19–32 in the Christian Bible, where John denies that he is the One and that the one who comes after him is Jesus, who gives life eternally.

69. Shenk, *Changing Frontiers of Mission*, 16.

living in the inner city, this meant the vile living conditions they were in at the time. For others, that event might be poverty or a "broken home." Whatever the event, Tupac insisted that people keep their heads up. Hopelessness occurs when one cannot imagine a different future. Tupac encouraged his audience to keep believing for a better day, and that heaven itself might have a "ghetto." Simply put, there is a place that will accept "us" as we are.

2. Tupac seeks after God's face in the midst of tension, ambiguity, and doubt. Tupac's song "So Many Tears" is the perfect example of this. Held in tension is the sin of his past life, the hurt of his current, and the ambiguity of this future—death could be immanent, but begging God to let him into heaven's door, Tupac pleads his case with God, and even in his chaos, he says a "sinner's prayer" throughout the track.[70] That is a profound sociotheological statement that is in pursuit of a theology that fits the context it originated from.

3. Tupac sees himself as a leader, but as a leader among/amidst, not from on high. Tupac struggled with his position as a leader—he was very young and not the typical older, grayer, adult leader that most expect to see as a leader. Thus, this created a problematic conundrum for Tupac with older adults—he is too young to lead. Right? No. Tupac had a lived theology while still creating that space to learn, grow, and develop with God in the post-soul context. He pushed for better, yet allowed voices to come alongside and

70. This is isolated in the background of the song and can be heard during the second and third chorus.

help. The Outlawz are one example of those oterh voices.

4. Tupac allows doubt, ambiguity, and the mystery of God to exist and just be. For many in a post-soul context, there is no assurance or guarantee of a bright future—especially given the current state of political affairs. Moreover, answers and theologies of celebration are unacceptable, invalid, and, in some cases, worthless for a post-soulist. Moving into the twenty-first century, a theological framework that emphasizes doubt, ambiguity, and a mysterious God is key. A God who is solvable, answerable, figurable, and quantifiable is not worth following nor seeking after; it would suggest we have answers and have the power. Why, then, would we need a God?

5. Tupac creates the space needed to question traditional, accepted, normative, and stilted forms of spirituality that have created a crystalized Christian faith in the image of Whiteness. The church must be the beacon of light that opens the door initially and reinvites the people to engage from their space and not from a preimagined space of "salvation." Tupac, utilizing Hip Hop, had the ability to just allow the questions to stream—often he would instigate the questioning. For too long Christianity has been a symbol of distrust, corruption, lies, sexual misconduct, and misappropriating Christ—Tupac says, let us start there and acknowledge the atrocities, seek forgiveness, and then create a new way, together. A solid missional church opens doors, doesn't argue for separating undocumented families at the border, cares for life from birth to death, realizes guns don't create peace, and helps the community they are working with; they do

> not decide for them or act in the place of God in their lives, but allow them to think for themselves, critically. To think for oneself, though, means to question. It is time we go there and Tupac can lead the way.

I think, to sum it up succinctly, Tupac is someone to be engaged with much like one would a Howard Thurman or a W. E. B. DuBois. This book only scratches the surface of the complexities someone like Tupac presents. But, that's good, right? We all like being left wanting more and Tupac is just that type of person. Whether you've been burned by fundamentalism, scorned by Bible-thumping people for being LGBTQ, or told there are only a few paths to God, Tupacian theology has space and room for all of that. It is a new way forward and provides a framework not for dogmatic procedures, but to growth, development, and nurturing the faith you feel and need to connect with God. That's post-soul. It's where we have to go, especially if we consider ourselves Christians. We often face seemingly difficult odds as faith develops and matures; Tupac points to a good bridge and pathway in these transitory periods.

4

A Few Concluding Thoughts

Like many who have grown up in Christian households, I was a product of the theology my parents gave me. My mom and grandmother (Dede) were my first theologians. They helped me interpret words I couldn't figure out while reading the King James Version. Dede couldn't speak English well, so I got an entirely different perspective on the Bible that I couldn't get from English. As a boy, I woke up early and read my Bible, using a red pencil to mark the passages I found interesting or that needed marking up. It's what my parents did, so I, in turn, did the same. My mom helped me with my daily devotional material and made me memorize Scripture. Dede was up at 5 a.m. every morning to pray and while that's just too damn early for even mice, I'd still pray the moment I woke up. That's what my parents did, so that's what I did. You get the picture. For most of us, our parents are our first entrance into God, faith, and church. That's all good and whatnot, but what about the questions, the doubt, and the material we can't explain? What about that time you did all the steps you were told to do, but you still didn't get that promotion, the jerk still got the promotion, those people still picked on you, and God still didn't intervene the way you were told? For someone who is Black like myself, I ask those questions a lot in the face of Black death seen on social media almost daily. I wonder what God was up to during the four hundred years of slavery and I question the existence of a God that is supposed to "save all" but has allowed so much shit to happen since Jesus left. I'm confounded. As much as I love my mom and Dede, they didn't have answers that made sense to me and at times didn't have answers at all. And, to be honest, I'm not sure anyone does. To be a Black man is to be in a constant state of anger and conflict here in the US; James Baldwin taught us that. I have come to realize that if I am going to continue this faith journey, I am going to have to go back to fifth and sixth century Africa to get at a non-colonized perspective on who God was and is for the Black people of today. Non-colonized Christian theology is hard to find—damn near impossible. My mom and Dede weren't prepared for these types of complexities, or, at the very least, didn't have the space to indulge in difficult questions. Dede lived a difficult life, left home young, only finished eighth grade, and worked service jobs all her life to make ends meet. My mom was a little better off, but with no college education and having had debilitating depression, she too worked hard and long hours. All this, to see me have a better life. To live good, and to raise a good family. I did and I am. I'm in debt to them eternally and I realize I have the privilege to be writing a book like this and spend the time pondering on post-soul this and postmodern that. That is why I continue to question and push forward and it is why I am encouraged to live in the tension they could not. Tupac has helped to give me the space to do that.

No, Tupac was not a singularized deity one worships and prays to; he'd even tell you to not do that. No, Tupac was not an Ivy League scholar with years of research behind him, but his knowledge and experience shaped him and his works. Tupac is not for everyone, but neither is evangelicalism. So, hopefully I've been able to, at the very least, carve out a better picture of him and his pursuits. His life was cut much too short.

This book has been concerned with Tupac Amaru Shakur and establishing his hermeneutical, ecclesiological, and numinous pursuits throughout his music, poetry, and life. In this book, I have said that Tupac was and is one of the only rappers within the Hip Hop community and continuum to who have earned, at least at the time of this research and publication, the title of "ghetto saint" and "urban prophet." Tupac's music searched through sexuality, manhood, pain, violence, revenge, hate, anger, love, hope, nihilism, and a pursuit of God in a contextualized manner. Tupac questions church and asks why traditions must continue if they don't make sense. Tupac was the externalized secular discussion of transmediated discourses of religious pursuits within the Hip Hop community. Tupac was and still is a prophetic and totemic symbol within Hip Hop and urban communities.

Tupac was still human, and contradictory to his own belief system at times. He wanted "peace," yet was passionately in a feud with Biggie Smalls, Sean Puffy Combs, and Nas—claiming on several occasions that he had "fucked Biggie's wife." Moreover, there was the issue of his own personal demons of insecurity, self-worth, and lack of stability, which gave Tupac an unsteady persona at times and an image in the public sphere that said he was just a "thug"—the literal definition and not the one Tupac had imagined with THUG LIFE.[1] This all embodies a faith and human

1. THUG LIFE means "The Hate U Give Little Infants Fucks Everyone."

experience not tolerated by many Christian contexts, yet Tupac's message was, at its core, a Judeo-Christian one. Where, then, does that leave us?

Even within this contradiction and seemingly hypocritical ethos, Tupac remains "prophetic" to many and creates that post-soul space for an unconventional missiology to take grip. It is because he was so transparent with his faults and shortcomings that made him into one of Hip Hop's most respected artists and voices. Perhaps it was because he intertwined God (the sacred), his own life (the secular), with a realist form of "life" in urban context (the profane) that made him into the ghetto theologian he was. Tupac's painful past might have given him the artistic insights to create music, poetry, and messages that could relate to his audience and within the Hip Hop continuum.

I think we have a long way to go before we reach consensus on what a Christian theology really is. I'm also concerned about the mounting hate from White nationalists and conservatives alike. Tupac eerily talked about a lot of this and how we as PoCs needed to unite at a much stronger level. Look, I'm not here to get too political or end-of-time-like—even though it's in my blood having been raised in a Seventh Day Adventist home. But I am here to suggest that maybe, just maybe, we don't have all the answers and pathways and that sometimes someone comes along who doesn't fit the mantra of a saint and offers up some tidbits of knowledge that may be able to help us. I think that person is my man Tupac. I hope this has helped in some way, and by all means, keep doubting, questioning, and living in the tension of life. Onward!

Attachment A

Pictorial View of Tupac

Attachment A

Attachment A

Attachment B

THUG LIFE Code

"I didn't create T.H.U.G. L.I.F.E., I diagnosed it."

– TUPAC SHAKUR

In 1992 at the "Truc Picnic" in Cali, Tupac was instrumental in getting rival members of the Crips and Bloods to sign the code of THUG LIFE. He and Mutulu Shakur had helped write up the code, with help from other "OGs."

The code of THUG LIFE is listed here. It details dos and don'ts for being a righteous thug and banger.

Code of THUG LIFE

1. All new Jacks to the game must know: a) He's going to get rich. b) He's going to jail. c) He's going to die.
2. Crew Leaders: You are responsible for legal/financial payment commitments to crew members; your word must be your bond.
3. One crew's rat is every crew's rat. Rats are now like a disease; sooner or later we all get it; and they should too.

4. Crew leader and posse should select a diplomat, and should work ways to settle disputes. In unity, there is strength!
5. Car jacking in our Hood is against the Code.
6. Slinging to children is against the Code.
7. Having children slinging is against the Code.
8. No slinging in schools.
9. Since the rat Nicky Barnes opened his mouth; ratting has become accepted by some. We're not having it.
10. Snitches is outta here.
11. The Boys in Blue don't run nothing; we do. Control the Hood, and make it safe for squares.
12. No slinging to pregnant Sisters. That's baby killing; that's genocide!
13. Know your target, who's the real enemy.
14. Civilians are not a target and should be spared.
15. Harm to children will not be forgiven.
16. Attacking someone's home where their family is known to reside, must be altered or checked.
17. Senseless brutality and rape must stop.
18. Our old folks must not be abused.
19. Respect our Sisters. Respect our Brothers.
20. Sisters in the Life must be respected if they respect themselves.
21. Military disputes concerning business areas within the community must be handled professionally and not on the block.
22. No shooting at parties.

23. Concerts and parties are neutral territories; no shooting!
24. Know the Code; it's for everyone.
25. Be a real ruff neck. Be down with the code of the THUG LIFE.
26. Protect yourself at all times.

Some Other Interpretations

THUG LIFE means: **T**he **H**ate **U** **G**ave **L**il **I**nfants **F**ucks **E**veryone

NIGGA means: **N**ever **I**gnorant **G**etting **G**oals **A**ccomplished

OUTLAW stands for: **O**perating **U**nder **T**hug **L**aws **A**s **W**arriors

MOB stands for: **M**ember **O**f **B**loods and/or **M**oney **O**ver **B**itches

Attachment C

Black Panther Ten-Point Program and Platform

1. WE WANT freedom. We want power to determine the destiny of our Black Community.

WE BELIEVE that black people will not be free until we are able to determine our destiny.

2. WE WANT full employment for our people.

WE BELIEVE that the federal government is responsible and obligated to give every man employment or a guaranteed income. We believe that if the white American businessmen will not give full employment, then the means of production should be taken from the businessmen and placed in the community so that the people of the community can organize and employ all of its people and give a high standard of living.

3. WE WANT an end to the robbery by the CAPITALIST of our Black Community.

WE BELIEVE that this racist government has robbed us and now we are demanding the overdue debt of forty acres and two mules. Forty acres and two mules were promised 100 years ago as restitution for slave labor and mass murder of black people. We will accept the payment in currency, which will be distributed, to our many communities. The Germans are now aiding the Jews in Israel for the genocide of the Jewish people. The Germans murdered six million Jews. The American racist has taken part in the slaughter of over fifty million black people; therefore, we feel that this is a modest demand that we make.

4. WE WANT decent housing, fit for the shelter of human beings.

WE BELIEVE that if the white landlords will not give decent housing to our black community, then the housing and the land should be made into cooperatives so that our community, with government aid, can build and make decent housing for its people.

5. WE WANT education for our people that exposes the true nature of this decadent American society. We want education that teaches us our true history and our role in the present-day society.

WE BELIEVE in an educational system that will give to our people knowledge of self. If a man does not have knowledge of himself and his position in society and the world, then he has little chance to relate to anything else.

6. WE WANT all black men to be exempt from military service.

WE BELIEVE that Black people should not be forced to fight in the military service to defend a racist government that does not protect us. We will not fight and kill other people of color in the world who, like black people, are being victimized by the white racist government of America. We will protect ourselves from the force and violence of the racist police and the racist military, by whatever means necessary.

7. WE WANT an immediate end to POLICE BRUTALITY and MURDER of black people.

WE BELIEVE we can end police brutality in our black community by organizing black self-defense groups that are dedicated to defending our black community from racist police oppression and brutality. The Second Amendment to the Constitution of the United States gives a right to bear arms. We therefore believe that all black people should arm themselves for self-defense.

8. WE WANT freedom for all black men held in federal, state, county, and city prisons and jails.

WE BELIEVE that all black people should be released from the many jails and prisons because they have not received a fair and impartial trial.

9. WE WANT all black people when brought to trial to be tried in court by a jury of their peer group or people from their black communities, as defined by the Constitution of the United States.

WE BELIEVE that the courts should follow the United States Constitution so that black people will receive fair trials. The 14th Amendment of the US Constitution gives a man a right to be tried by his peer group. A peer is a person from a similar economic, social, religious, geographical, environmental, historical and racial background. To do this the court will be forced to select a jury from the black community from which the black defendant came. We have been, and are being tried by all-white juries that have no understanding of the "average reasoning man" of the black community.

10. WE WANT land, bread, housing, education, clothing, justice and peace. And as our major political objective, a United Nations supervised plebiscite to be held throughout the black colony in which only black colonial subjects will be allowed to participate, for the purpose of determining the will of black people as to their national destiny.

Attachment C

WHEN, in the course of human events, it becomes necessary for one people to dissolve the political bonds which have connected them with another, and to assume, among the powers of the earth, the separate and equal station to which the laws of nature and nature's God entitle them, a decent respect to the opinions of mankind requires that they should declare the causes which impel them to the separation.

WE HOLD these truths to be self-evident, that all men are created equal; that they are endowed by their Creator with certain inalienable rights; that among these are life, liberty, and the pursuit of happiness. **That, to secure these rights, governments are instituted among men, deriving their just powers from the consent of the governed; that, whenever any form of government becomes destructive of these ends, it is the right of the people to alter or abolish it, and to institute a new government, laying its foundation on such principles, and/or organizing its powers in such form, as to them shall seem most likely to effect their safety and happiness.**Prudence, indeed, will dictate that governments long established should not be changed for light and transient causes; and, accordingly, all experience hath shown, that mankind are more disposed to suffer, while evils are sufferable, than to right themselves by abolishing the forms to which they are accustomed. **But, when a long train of abuses and usurpations, pursuing invariably the same object, evinces a design to reduce them under absolute despotism, it is their right, it is their duty, to throw off such government, and to provide new guards for their future security.**[1]

1. Taken from http://www.itsabouttimebpp.com/home/bpp_program_platform.html.

Attachment D

Tupac's Tattoos

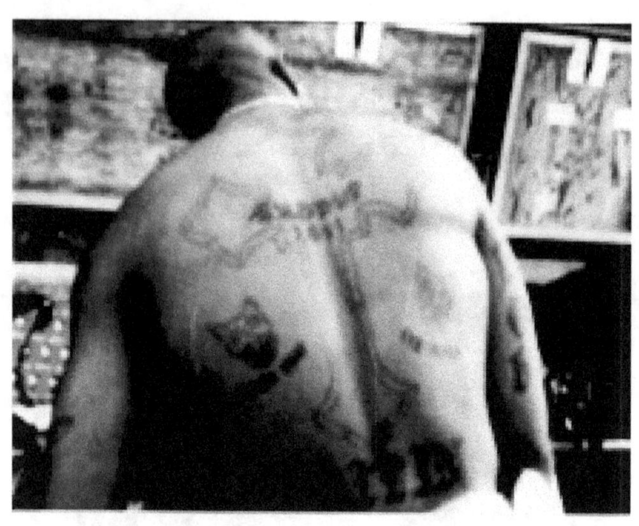

Tupac's Chest	Top Left: 2pac Top Right: Queen Neferetete (Egyptian Queen) with "2.DIE.4" below it. Middle: A machine gun and the words "50 Niggaz." Stomach: The words "Thug Life," with a bullet as the "i."
Tupac's Arms	Left Shoulder: Panther head Left Upper Arm: Jesus' head on a burning cross. Off to the left of the cross it says, "Only God can judge me." On his left inner arm is written "Trust Nobody." Left Forearm: The word "Outlaw," underneath which is another "crown" that you can see in the movie "Gang Related." Right Shoulder: The word "westside." Right Upper Arm: Skull and crossbones. Under the word "heartless." Under the skull and crossbones written in small print it says, "My only fear of death is coming back reincarnated." Right Forearm: Written in old English lettering, the word "Notorious." Back Arm: On the back of the arm it says "MOB."
Tupac's Neck	Right Side: In the movie "Gang Related" and "Gridlocked" you will see the name "Machiavelli." Back Side: There is a Crown and then under that is the word "Playaz." Under "Playaz" are the words "Fuck the World."

Tupac's Back	A big cross is on his back with the word "Exodus 18:11," meaning, "Now I know that the lord is greater than all gods: for in the things wherein they dealt proudly he was above them" in the middle of the cross. On each side of the cross is a clown mask. The mask on his right is crying and underneath it says "cry later." The other mask on his left side is smiling and it says, "smile now." Under the cross is a big word saying "Ballin."

Attachment E

Tupac's Musical Connection to Slave Music

Tupac's Song	Slave Narrative and Song Parallel	Black Popular Culture (BPC) Value
"Young Black Male"	"Looked Down De Road"	In both of these songs, the artists make the connection with survival, the struggle for survival, and the power to survive; especially for young Blacks. The pain is much, and the sorrow is plentiful, but if we can just hold on together, we can make it happen.
"Cradle to Tha Grave"	"By and By I'm Goin' to See Them"	In these two parallel songs, both Pac and the slaves discuss the pain of loved ones gone. "Well, mournin' time will soon be over" is the same theme that Pac uses in his song when he says, "All my homies drinkin liquor, tears in everybody's eyes. Niggaz cried, to mourn a homie's homicide." In these two songs we see the connection to death, accepting death, but wishing that loved ones would not have to pass. A theme that is seen in many other songs within BPC as well.

Tupac's Song	Slave Narrative and Song Parallel	Black Popular Culture (BPC) Value
"Death Around The Corner"	"Ain't That Good News?"	Both of these songs deal with the ultimate rest, happiness, and life struggle: death. In the inner city, many youth see death as the ultimate resting place and a time of peace, at last. Death is glorified, the slave knew this too. The "Good-News" for the slave, was heaven and God, i.e., death. For Tupac, this was the same. He wanted to leave the "messed up earth" and return home to his father in heaven. "Tryin to keep it together, no one lives forever anyway. Strugglin and strivin, my destiny's to die."
"Heaven Ain't Too Hard 2 Find"	"Marching Up the Heavenly Road"	In both of these songs, the narrative changes for hope and peace; in a journey that will end in heaven for those who wait. The slave narrative says, "O come a-long_Mos-es, don't get lost, Marching up the Heavenly road." Don't lose hope or vision, your pain and suffering will be rewarded, is the ultimate message for the listener. Tupac infused many of his songs with this same message. In this particular song, he encourages the listener to be ready and to hold on: "Heaven ain't too hard to find, you just gotta have faith."

This is derived and connected to Howard Odum's *Negro and His Songs* (1968) and Mark Fisher's work, *Negro Slave Songs* (1969), in which both scholars look at Black and slave songs. I make the connection to Tupac's music.

The song "Hold On Just a Little While Longer" also parallels Tupac's message:

Hold On Just a Little While Longer

Hold on, just a little while longer
Hold on, just a little while longer
Hold on, just a little while longer
Everything will be alright
Everything will be alright

Pray on, just a little while longer
Pray on, just a little while longer
Pray on, just a little while longer
Everything will be alright
Everything will be alright

Fight on, just a little while longer
Fight on, just a little while longer
Fight on, just a little while longer
Everything will be alright
Everything will be alright

Attachment F

Song: "So Many Tears"

I shall not fear no man but God
Though I walk through the valley of death
I shed so many tears (if I should die before I wake)
Please God walk with me (grab a nigga and take me to Heaven)

Back in elementary, I thrived on misery
Left me alone I grew up amongst a dyin breed
Inside my mind couldn't find a place to rest
until I got that Thug Life tatted on my chest
Tell me can you feel me? I'm not livin in the past, you wanna last
Be tha first to blast, remember Kato
No longer with us he's deceased
Call on the sirens, seen him murdered in the streets
Now rest in peace
Is there heaven for a G? Remember me
So many homies in the cemetery, shed so many tears

Ahh, I suffered through the years, and shed so many tears.
Lord, I lost so many peers, and shed so many tears

Now that I'm strugglin in this business, by any means
Label me greedy gettin green, but seldom seen
And fuck the world cause I'm cursed, I'm havin visions

of leavin here in a hearse, God can you feel me?
Take me away from all the pressure, and all the pain
Show me some happiness again, I'm goin blind
I spend my time in this cell, ain't livin well
I know my destiny is Hell, where did I fail?
My life is in denial, and when I die,
baptized in eternal fire I'll shed so many tears

Lord, I suffered through the years, and shed so many tears.
Lord, I lost so many peers, and shed so many tears

Now I'm lost and I'm weary, so many tears
I'm suicidal, so don't stand near me
My every move is a calculated step, to bring me closer
to embrace an early death, now there's nothin left
There was no mercy on the streets, I couldn't rest
I'm barely standin, bout to go to pieces, screamin peace
And though my soul was deleted, I couldn't see it
I had my mind full of demons tryin to break free
They planted seeds and they hatched, sparkin the flame
inside my brain like a match, such a dirty game
No memories, just a misery
Paintin a picture of my enemies killin me, in my sleep
Will I survive til the mo'nin, to see the sun
Please Lord forgive me for my sins, cause here I come.

Lord, I suffered through the years (God) and shed so many tears.
God, I lost so many peers, and shed so many tears

Lord knows I tried, been a witness to homicide
Seen drivebys takin lives, little kids die
Wonder why as I walk by
Broken-hearted as I glance at the chalk line, gettin high
This ain't the life for me, I wanna change
But ain't no future right for me, I'm stuck in the game
I'm trapped inside a maze

See this Tanqueray influenced me to gettin crazy
Disillusioned lately, I've been really wantin babies
so I could see a part of me that wasn't always shady
Don't trust my lady, cause she's a product of this poison
I'm hearin noises, think she fuckin all my boys, can't take no more
I'm fallin to the floor; beggin for the Lord to let me in
to Heaven's door—shed so many tears
(Dear God, please let me in)

Lord, I've lost so many years, and shed so many tears.
I lost so many peers, and shed so many tears
Lord, I suffered through the years, and shed so many tears.
God, I lost so many peers, and shed so many tears

Attachment G

Material Used in Tupac's Ethnolifehistory

Below are the listings of materials used in Tupac's ethnolifehistory

Archival DVDs	**Poetry**	**Interview Audio CDs**	**Other**
1) Tupac Vs. 2) Thug Angel 3) Tupac Shakur: 4) Before I wake 5) Tupac Resurrection 6) 2Pac: Hip Hop Genius 7) Apprentice of Tupac Shakur	1) The Rose That Grew From Concrete 2) Tupac Legacy (Volume 1)	1) Tupac Shakur Speaks 2) Davey D 1992 Interview 3) 450 hours of interviews found on YouTube 4) 500 hours of interviews given to me on CD	1) The Rose that Grew from Concrete (CD) various artists; Volume 1 2) The Rose that Grew from Concrete (CD) various artists' Volume 2

All eighteen published CDs were used to study Tupac's music.

Attachment H

Tupac's Involvement with the Law

Date	Event
December 1992	Tupac files a $10 million lawsuit against the Oakland Police for alleged police brutality following an arrest for jaywalking.
April 1992	Ronald Ray Howard, 19, shoots a Texas State Trooper and Howard's attorney claims that the young man was incited by Tupac's album *2Pacalypse Now*, which was in the tape deck at the time. Vice president Dan Quayle denounces Tupac and firmly states that his album has no place in our society.
August 1992	Tupac has an altercation with some old friends in Marin City, which results in the death of a six-year-old bystander and the arrest of Tupac's half brother, Maurice Harding, who was eventually released due to the lack of evidence.
March 1993	Tupac gets into a fight with a limo drive who accused Tupac of using drugs in his car. Tupac was arrested but the charges were later dropped.
April 1993	Tupac was arrested again for taking a swing with a baseball bat at a local rapper during a concert. He was sentenced to ten days in prison.

Tupac's Involvement with the Law

Date	Event
October 1993	Tupac is arrested for allegedly shooting at two off-duty Atlanta police officers who were allegedly harassing Black motorists. The charges were later dropped. Columbia Pictures forces director John Singleton to drop Tupac from his upcoming film *Higher Learning*. Tupac gets into an altercation with *Menace II Society's* director Allen Hughes.
November 1993	A nineteen-year-old woman accuses Tupac of sexual assault.
March 1994	Tupac begins serving a fifteen-day prison sentence for punching director Allen Hughes after he was dropped from the motion picture *Menace II Society.*
September 1994	Two Milwaukee teens murder a police officer and cite Tupac's song "Souljah's Story" as their inspiration.
November 1994	Tupac's sexual assault trial opens.
November 30, 1994	While entering the lobby of the Quad Recording Studios in Times Square, New York City, Tupac is shot five times and robbed of jewels and cash estimated to be worth over $50,000.
November 1994	Tupac is acquitted of sodomy and weapons charges but found guilty of sexual abuse.
February 14, 1995	Tupac begins serving his eighteen-month to four-and-a-half-year sentence in New York's Rikers Island Penitentiary.

Attachment I

Tupac's Variety of Interviews

- Prison interview (1995); Source: Vibe Magazine
- Tupac as a teenager (circa 1988); Source: Unknown
- Tupac discussing his frustration with Biggie Smalls (circa 1996); Source: unknown
- Tupac with Tabitha Soren from MTV (1993–1996); Source: MTV (multiple interviews and specials put on by MTV)
- Tupac discussing Thug Life (circa 1993); Source: Vibe magazine with VH-1 interviewer
- Tupac discussing the "King of Niggadom" (circa early 1996); Source: unknown
- Tupac Christmas Interview (1995); Source: MTV interviewer
- Tupac discusses church, God, the illuminati (circa 1994); Source: Vibe magazine
- Tupac deposition (1993, 1994, and 1995); Source: unknown
- Tupac discusses his anxiety, the real reason he was angry with Biggie, and his thoughts about leaving Death Row (late 1996); Source: Unknown, given to the author on tape

- Tupac BET interview (believed 1995); Source: Ed Gordon interviewer
- Tupac discusses his vision and plans to create a Hip Hop political candidate by the year 2000 (believed mid-1996); Source: Unknown, tape given to author

Bibliography

Alper, Garth. "Making Sense Out of Postmodern Music?" *Popular Music and Society* 24 (Winter 2000) 1–14.

Althaus-Reid, Marcella. *Indecent Theology: Theological Perversions in Sex, Gender, and Politics*. New York: Routledge, 2000.

Anderson, Raymond D S. "Black Beats for One People; Causes and Effects of Identification with Hip-Hop Culture." PhD. diss., Regent University, 2003.

Bauman, Zygmunt. "Postmodern Religion?" In *Religion, Modernity, and Postmodernity*, edited by Paul Heelas, 55–78. Malden, MA: Blackwell, 1998.

Best, Steven, and Douglas Kellner. *Postmodern Theory: Critical Interrogations*. New York: Guilford, 1991.

Betts, Raymond. *A History of Popular Culture: More of Everything, Faster, and Brighter*. New York: Routledge, 2004.

Block, Fred, et al. "The Compassion Gap in American Poverty Policy." *Contexts* 5 (2006) 14–20.

Boyd, Todd. *Am I Black Enough for You? Popular Culture from the 'Hood and Beyond*. Bloomington: Indiana University Press, 1997.

———. *The H.N.I.C.: The Death of Civil Rights and the Reign of Hip Hop*. New York: New York University Press, 2002.

Cavazzini, Emma. *Art of the 20th Century*. Neo-Avant-Gardes, Postmodern and Global Art 4. Milano, Italy: Skira, 2009.

Chang, Jeff. *Can't Stop Won't Stop: A History of the Hip Hop Generation*. New York: St. Martin's Press, 2005.

Cone, James H. *Black Theology and Black Power*. 5th ed. Maryknoll, NY: Orbis, 1997.

———. *A Black Theology of Liberation*. 20th ed. Maryknoll, NY: Orbis, 1990.

———. "The Blues: A Secular Spiritual." In *Sacred Music of the Secular City: From Blues to Rap*, edited by Jon Michael Spencer, 68–97. Durham: Duke University Press, 1992.

———. *God of the Oppressed*. Maryknoll, NY: Orbis, 1997.

Costen, Melva Wilson. "Protest and Praise: Sacred Music of Black Religion by Jon Michael Spencer, Minneapolis, Fortress, 1990." *Theology Today* 48 (October 1, 1991) 360–62.

Covert, Tawnya Adkins. "Consumption and Citizenship During the Second World War." *Journal of Consumer Culture* 3 (November 1, 2003) 315–42.

Cox, Harvey. *Religion in the Secular City: Toward a Postmodern Theology*. New York: Simon & Schuster, 1984.

Cupitt, Don. "Post-Christianity." In *Religion, Modernity, and Postmodernity*, edited by Paul Heelas, 218–32. Malden, MA: Blackwell, 1998.

Datcher, Michael, Kwame Alexander, and Mutulu Shakur. *Tough Love: The Life and Death of Tupac Shakur, Cultural Criticism and Familial Observations.* Alexandria, VA: Alexander Pub., 1997.

Dyson, Michael Eric. *Between God and Gangsta Rap: Bearing Witness to Black Culture.* New York: Oxford University Press, 1996.

———. *Holler If You Hear Me: Searching for Tupac Shakur.* New York: Basic Civitas, 2001.

———. *Is Bill Cosby Right? Or Has the Black Middle Class Lost Its Mind?* New York: Basic Civitas, 2005.

Edwards, Herbert O. "Black Theology: Retrospect and Prospect." *Journal of Religious Thought* 32 (1975) 46–59.

Emerson, Michael O., and Christian Smith. *Divided by Faith: Evangelical Religion and the Problem of Race in America.* Oxford: Oxford University Press, 2001.

Fisher, Mark Miles. *Negro Slave Songs in the United States.* New York: Citadel, 1969.

Floyd, Samuel A. *The Power of Black Music: Interpreting Its History from Africa to the United States.* New York: Oxford University Press, 1995.

Forman, Murray. *The 'Hood Comes First: Race, Space, and Place in Rap and Hip-Hop.* Middletown: Wesleyan University Press, 2002.

Freire, Paulo. *Pedagogy of the Oppressed.* Translated by Myra Bergman Ramos. 30th anniversary ed. New York: Continuum, 2000.

George, Nelson. *Buppies, B-Boys, Baps & Bohos: Notes on Post-Soul Black Culture.* 1st ed. New York: Harper Collins, 1992.

———. *Hiphop America.* New York: Penguin, 1998.

———. *Post-Soul Nation: The Explosive, Contradictory, Triumphant, and Tragic 1980s as Experienced by African Americans (Previously Known as Blacks and Before That Negroes).* New York: Viking, 2004.

George, Nelson, and National Urban League. *Stop the Violence: Overcoming Self Destruction*. New York: Pantheon Books, 1990.

Hall, John R. "The Capitals of Cultures: A Nonholistic Approach to Status Situations, Class, Gender, and Ethnicity." In *Cultivating Differences*, edited by M. Lamount and A. Fournier, 257–85. Chicago: Chicago University Press, 1992.

Hall, Staurt. "What Is This 'Black' in Black Popular Culture?." In *Black Popular Culture*, edited by Michele Wallace and Gina Dent, 21–33. New York: Dia Center for the Arts, New Press, 1998.

Hassan, Ihab. "Postmodernism: A Paracritical Bibliography." In *From Modernism to Postmodernism: An Anthology*, edited by Lawrence Cahoone, 382–400. Malden, MA: Blackwell, 1996.

Hattery, Angela J., and Earl Smith. *African American Families*. Thousand Oaks, CA: Sage, 2007.

Heidegger, Martin. "Letter on Humanism." In *From Modernism to Postmodernism: An Anthology*, edited by Lawrence Cahoone, 274–308. Malden, MA: Blackwell, 1996.

Hodge, Daniel White. *Heaven Has a Ghetto: The Missiological Gospel & Theology of Tupac Amaru Shakur*. Saarbrucken, Germany: VDM Verlag Dr. Muller Academic, 2009.

———. *Hip Hop's Hostile Gospel: A Post-Soul Theological Exploration*. Center for Critical Research on Religion and Harvard University. Edited by Warren Goldstein. Vol. 6. Boston: Brill Academic, 2017.

———. "Insights from Tupac Amaru Shakur for Youth Workers." *Fuller Youth Institute* 2.2 (n.y.) 1–22.

———. "No Church in the Wild: An Ontology of Hip Hop's Socio-Religious Discourse in Tupac's 'Black Jesuz.'" *Nomos* 10 (March 23, 2013) 1–5.

———. "No Church in the Wild: Hip Hop Theology & Mission." *Missiology: An International Review* XL.4 (2013) 1–13.

———. *The Soul of Hip Hop: Rimbs Timbs & a Cultural Theology*. Downers Grove, IL: InterVarsity, 2010.

Iverem, Esther. "The Politics of 'Fuck It' and the Passion to Be a Free Black." In *Tough Love: The Life and Death of Tupac Shakur*, edited by Michael Datcher and Kwame Alexander, 41–47. Alexandria, VA: Black Words Books, 1997.

Jospeh, Jamal. *Tupac Shakur: Legacy*. New York: Atria, 2006.

Kain & Abel. "Black Jesus." Featuring and Master P. On *The 7 Sins*. Priority Records, 1996, compact disc.

Kirk-Duggan, Cheryl A. "The Theo-Poetic Theological Ethics of Lauryn Hill and Tupac Shakur." In *Creating Ourselves: African*

Americans and Hispanic Americans on Popular Culture and Religious Expression, edited by Anthony B. Pinn and Benjamín Valentín, 204–23. Durham: Duke University Press, 2009.

Kitwana, Bakari. *The Hip Hop Generation: Young Blacks and the Crisis in African-American Culture.* New York: Basic Civitas, 2003.

Lash, Scott. "Postmodernism as Humanism? Urban Space and Social Theory." In *Theories of Modernity and Postmodernity*, edited by Bryan S. Turner, 45–61. Thousand Oaks, CA: Sage, 1990.

———. *Sociology of Posmodernism.* New York: Routledge, 1990.

Lazin, Lauren. *Tupac: Resurrection.* USA: MTV Films & Amaru Entertainment, 2003.

Lincoln, Eric C., and Lawrence H. Mamiya. *The Black Church in the African American Experience.* Durham: Duke University Press, 1990.

Major, Brenda, Alison Blodorn, and Gregory Major Blascovich. "The Threat of Increasing Diversity: Why Many White Americans Support Trump in the 2016 Presidential Election." *Group Processes & Intergroup Relations* 21 (2018) 931–40.

Miles, Jack. *Christ: A Crisis in the Life of God.* New York: Alfred A. Knopf, 2001.

Moss, Otis. "Real Big: The Hip Hop Pastor as Postmodern Prophet." In *The Gospel Remix: Reaching the Hip Hop Generation*, edited by Ralph Watkins, 110–38. Valley Forge, PA: Judson, 2007.

Neal, Mark Anthony. "Sold Out on Soul: The Corporate Annexation of Black Popular Music." *Popular Music and Society* 21 (Fall 1997) 117–35.

———. *Soul Babies: Black Popular Culture and the Post-Soul Aesthetic.* New York: Routledge, 2002.

———. *What the Music Said: Black Popular Music and Black Public Culture.* New York: Routledge, 1999.

Odum, Howard W. *The Negro and His Songs: A Study of Typical Negro Songs in the South.* 306 vols. Westport, CT: Negro Universities Press, 1968.

Oliver, William. "'The Streets.'" *Journal of Black Studies* 36 (2006): 918-37.

Otto, Rudolph. *The Idea of the Holy.* 2nd ed. London: Oxford University Press, 1950.

Peralta, Stacy. *Crips and Bloods: Made in America.* 93 minutes. USA: Verso Entertainment, 2008.

Peters, Ken, dir. *Tupac Vs.* 90 minutes. USA: Dennon Entertainment, 2001, film.

Pinn, Anthony. *The Black Church in the Post-civil Rights Era.* Maryknoll, NY: Orbis, 2002.

———. *Embodiment and the New Shape of Black Theology.* Religion, Race, and Ethnicity. New York: New York University Press, 2010.

———. *Why Lord? Suffering and Evil in Black Theology.* New York: Continuum, 1995.

Potter, Russell A. *Spectacular Vernaculars: Hip-Hop and the Politics of Postmodernism.* New York: State University of New York Press, 1995.

Powery, Luke A. *Spirit Speech: Lament and Celebration in Preaching.* Nashville: Abingdon, 2009.

Reed, Teresa L. *The Holy Profane: Religion in Black Popular Music.* Lexington: The University Press of Kentucky, 2003.

Renaud, Myriam. "Myths Debunked: Why Did White Evangelical Christians Vote for Trump?" The Martin Marty Center for the Advanced Study of Religion, The University of Chicago, 2017. https://divinity.uchicago.edu/sightings/myths-debunked-why-did-white-evangelical-christians-vote-trump.

Ruskin, Matt. *The Hip Hop Project.* 85 minutes. USA: Pressure Point Films; Image Entertainment; One Village Entertainment, 2009.

Shakur, Tupac. *The Rose That Grew from Concrete.* New York: Pocket Books, 1999.

Shakur, Tupac, et al. *Tupac: Resurrection, 1971–1996.* 1st Atria Books hardcover ed. New York: Atria, 2003.

Shenk, Wilbert R. *Changing Frontiers of Mission.* American Society of Missiology Series 28. Maryknoll, NY: Orbis, 1999.

Sides, Josh. *L.A. City Limits: African American Los Angeles from the Great Depression to the Present.* Berkeley and Los Angeles: University of California Press, 2003.

Slobin, Mark, and Jeff Todd Titon. "The Music-Culture as a World of Music." In *Worlds of Music: An Introduction to the Music of the World's Peoples*, edited by Jeff Todd Titon et al., 1–11. New York: Schirmer, 1984.

Smith, Efrem, and Phil Jackson. *The Hip Hop Church: Connecting with the Movement Shaping Our Culture.* Downers Grove, IL: InterVarsity, 2005.

Smith, Gregory A., and Jessica Martínez. "How the Faithful Voted: A Preliminary 2016 Analysis." Fact Tank: News in the Numbers, Pew Research Center, 2016. https://www.pewresearch.org/fact-tank/2016/11/09/how-the-faithful-voted-a-preliminary-2016-analysis/.

Spencer, Jon Michael. *Theological Music: An Introduction to Theomusicology*. Contributions to the Study of Music and Dance. New York: Greenwood, 1991.

Spirer, Peter. *Thug Angel: The Life of An Outlaw*. 92 minutes. USA: QD3 Entertainment, 2002.

Stark, Rodney Bainbridge Sims. *The Future of Religion : Secularization, Revival and Cult Formation [in English]*. Bekerley, Los Angeles, London: University of California press, 1985.

Taylor, Paul C. "Post-Black, Old Black." *African American Review* 41 (Winter 2007) 625–40.

Thurman, Howard. *Jesus and the Disinherited*. Boston: Beacon, 1976.

Valentín, Benjamín. "Tracings: Sketching the Cultural Geographies of Laino/a Theology." In *Creating Ourselves: African Americans and Hispanic Americans on Popular Culture and Religious Expression*, edited by Anthony B. Pinn and Benjamín Valentín, 38–61. Durham: Duke University Press, 2009.

West, Cornel. "The New Cultural Politics of Difference." In *Out There: Marginalization and Contemporary Culture*, edited by Russell Ferguson, 19–36. Cambridge: MIT Press, 1990.

———. *Prophetic Thought in Postmodern Times: Beyond Eurocentrism and Multiculturalism*. Vol. 1, Monroe, ME: Common Courage Press, 1993.

White, Armond. *Rebel for the Hell of It: The Life of Tupac Shakur*. New ed. New York: Thunder's Mouth, 2002.

White, Russell Christopher. "Constructions of Identity and Community in Hip-Hop Nationalism with Specific Reference to Public Enemy and Wu-Tang Clan." PhD diss., University of Southampton, 2002.

Whitesell, John, dir. *Malibu's Most Wanted*. Los Angeles: Warner Bros, 2003, film.

Wiese, Andrew. *Places of Their Own: African American Suburbanization in the Twentieth Century*. Historical Studies of Urban America. Chicago: University of Chicago, 2004.